APPLE WATCH SERIES 9 USER GUIDE

A Complete Step-By-Step Manual for Novices and Seasoned Users on Mastering Apple Watch Set Up and Navigation, Packed with Tips and Tricks

By

Ethan Quill

TABLE OF CONTENT

INTRODUCTION

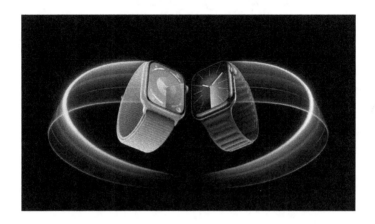

Introducing the latest features of Apple Watch and watchOS 10 with the introduction of Apple Watch Series 9. Equipped with the new S9 SiP chip, this edition offers improved display brightness and helps you track your lost iPhone with Precision Finding for iPhone.

Upgraded Interface

Get the most out of your Apple Watch display and experience an updated interface that lets you see more information at a glance. watchOS 10 introduces redesigned apps, smart stacks, and innovative navigation options.

Introducing the Smart Stack

Rotate the Digital Crown to reveal widgets to access relevant information from any watch face. Open Control Center to find a convenient way to view your recent apps. Press the side button on the watch face or any app to open Control Center, then double-click the digital crown to unhide the app switcher.

Easy Gestures and Controls

Double-tap the clock hand with your index finger and thumb at the same time to play/pause music, answer calls, stop the timer, and more.

New Dials

Enjoy new dials, including a combination of Snoopy and Woodstock, and a solar analog that lights up at night to improve readability. The palette indicates time with color changes throughout the day.

Outdoor Activities

Expand your outdoor activities with maps that provide detailed information on trails near you in the US, including names, lengths, times, photos, and more.

Apple Watch SE and Series 6 and later include new compass elevation and waypoint features. Track waypoints and altitudes and receive notifications about specific altitudes.

Fitness Privileges

Cyclists benefit from enhanced training and can automatically connect to Bluetooth-enabled accessories for additional metrics. See your functional threshold power estimates and seamlessly stream your cycling workouts to your iPhone for a comprehensive view.

Fitness+ subscribers have access to customized plans that tailor their workouts to their personal preferences. Stack multiple workouts and meditations for seamless transitions between activities.

Stay connected with friends with live location sharing in Messages and provide real-time updates on your whereabouts.

Music and More

Get recommended music and podcasts on your Apple Watch near Home Pod and see media suggestions in your smart stack.

SET UP YOUR APPLE

WATCH

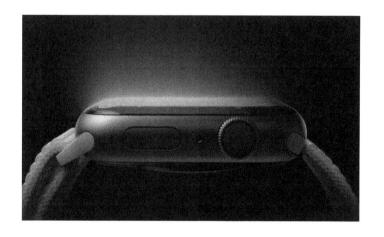

Pair your Apple Watch with your iPhone

To use your Apple Watch, you need to pair it with your iPhone. The iPhone and Apple Watch setup wizards work together to guide you through the pairing and setup process.

Requirements

To use Apple Watch Series 4 or later with watchOS 10, you must pair it with an iPhone Xs or later running iOS 17 or later.

Before you begin

Make sure your iPhone is updated to the latest iOS version. Open the Settings app, tap General, then tap Software Update. Make sure your iPhone's Bluetooth is turned on and connected to Wi-Fi or your cellular network. Swipe down from the top-right corner of your iPhone screen to access Control Center and make sure the

Bluetooth and Wi-Fi (or cellular) buttons are enabled.

Step 1: Power on and pair your Apple Watch

1. Place Apple Watch on your wrist to ensure a comfortable fit.
2. Press and hold the side button on your Apple Watch until you see the Apple logo.
3. If your Apple Watch won't turn on, charge the battery.
4. Place your iPhone near your Apple Watch, wait until the iPhone pairing screen appears, then tap Next. Or,

open the Apple Watch app on your

iPhone and tap Pair New Watch.

5. Tap Set Up for Me and follow the

onscreen instructions to position

your iPhone so your Apple Watch is

in the viewfinder. This will pair your

device.

Step 2: Set up your Apple Watch

If this is your first Apple Watch, tap Set

up Apple Watch and follow the

instructions for both devices to complete

setup. - If you've been using another

Apple Watch with your iPhone, you can

make it your new Apple Watch, or tap

Customize Settings to customize your setup.

Follow the onscreen instructions to:

1. Enter your Apple ID and password.

2. Create a passcode (standard or long).

3. Customize text size, personal information, and health notifications.

Step 3: Enable Cellular Service

If your Apple Watch supports cellular, you can enable it during setup or later in the Apple Watch app on your iPhone.

Make sure both devices are using the same mobile phone provider.

Note: Cell phone service availability varies by region.

Step 4: Keep your device nearby while syncing

Once the pairing process is complete, a watch face appears on your Apple Watch, indicating it's ready to use.

Charging your Apple Watch

Charger setup

1. Place the charger or charging cable in a well-ventilated area on a flat surface.

2. Use the included Apple Watch Magnetic Fast Charging to USB-C Cable (for Series 7, 8, and 9) or Magnetic Charging Cable (for other models). You can also use the MagSafe Duo charger or magnetic charging dock (sold separately).

3. Connect the cable to the power adapter (sold separately).

4. Plug the adapter into a power outlet. For fast charging, use an 18W or higher USB-C power adapter.

Start charging

1. Place the charging cable on the back of your Apple Watch and make sure it's oriented correctly.

2. A beep (except in silent mode) and a charging symbol on the dial confirm charging.

3. The icon will turn red when the watch needs power and green when charging. Displayed in yellow in power saving mode.

You can charge the watch flat or horizontally depending on your preference.

To check the remaining amount:

- Press the side button to open the control center or add additional battery features to your watch face for easy checking.

Save energy:

Enable power saving mode to extend battery life. This disables certain features such as Always On Display and background measurements.

1. Press the side button to open Control Center.
2. Tap Battery Percentage to turn on power saving mode.

Note: Power saving mode will turn off after 80% charge.

Return to normal power mode:

Press the side button to open Control Center and tap Battery Percentage to turn off power saving mode.

Check the time since last charge:

Open the Settings app and tap Battery to see battery percentage, usage graphs, and last charge information.

Check the battery status:

To assess your Apple Watch's battery capacity compared to when it was new, open the Settings app, tap Battery, then tap Battery Health.

Battery charging optimization:

Extend battery life by enabling optimized battery charging in battery settings.

Prevent background app updates:

Save battery by turning off Background app refresh in General > Background app refresh. Turn it off globally or for individual apps.

Turn Apple Watch On Or Off

Turn on:

If your Apple Watch is turned off, press the side button until you see the Apple logo (you may see a brief black screen initially). A clock face appears, indicating that your Apple Watch is turned on.

Note: If your Apple Watch won't turn on, make sure it's charging or try a force restart.

Erase:

However, we recommend that you keep your Apple Watch powered on at all times. However, if you need to turn them off, follow these steps:

1. Press and hold the side button until the slider appears.
2. Tap the power button on the top right.

3. Slide the power off slider to the right.

When your Apple Watch is turned off, press and hold the Digital Crown to view the time. You can't turn off your Apple Watch while it's charging. First, unplug the charger.

Always-on feature:

On compatible Apple Watch models (Series 5, 6, 7, 8, and 9), the Always On feature lets you see the watch face and time even when your wrist is down. It works perfectly when I raise my wrist.

To enable Always On:

1. Open the Settings app on your Apple Watch.

2. Tap Display & Brightness, then tap Always On.

3. Enable "Always On" and set options such as "Show complications data", "Show notifications", "Show apps", etc.

Note: Always On is disabled in power saving mode. Tap the display to see the watch face in power-saving mode.

Start display:

You can activate your Apple Watch display as follows:

1. Raise your wrist (lower it to go
    back to sleep).

2. Tap the display or press the
    Digital Crown.

3. Turn the digital crown up.

To customize alarm options:

1. Open the Settings app on your
    Apple Watch.

2. Go to Display & Brightness.

3. Disable "Wake on Wrist Raise" and
    "Wake On Crown Rotation" if
    desired.

Tip: To prevent your Apple Watch from momentarily waking up when you raise your wrist, use Theater Mode.

If your Apple Watch doesn't start up as expected, check your wrist and watch orientation settings, or make sure it has enough power.

Return to dial:

Choose when your Apple Watch returns to the watch face from open apps.

1. Open the Settings app on your Apple Watch.

2. Go to General > Return to Clock.

3. Select Always, After 2 minutes, or After 1 hour.

4. Alternatively, you can press the Digital Crown to return to the watch face.

Note: You can adjust the return time for individual apps.

Wake up to the last activity:

Certain apps can be set to pick up where you left off when your watch goes to sleep. For applicable apps:

1. Open the Settings app on your Apple Watch.

2. Go to General > Return to Clock.

3. Tap the app and enable Return to app.

To return to the watch face, stop your current activity in the app.

Leave the display on longer:

Extend the display time when you start up your Apple Watch.

1. Open the Settings app on your Apple Watch.
2. Tap Display & Brightness.
3. Tap Wake up time and select 70 seconds wake up.

Apple Watch Interactions: Basic Gestures

When combined with the digital crown and side button, Apple Watch provides intuitive control through these basic gestures:

Tap: Gently touch the screen with one finger.

Swipe: Easily move your finger in any direction on the screen, up, down, left, or right.

Drag: Move your finger seamlessly across the screen without lifting your finger for smooth navigation on the

screen.

WATCH AND FAMILY

Set up your family's Apple Watch

You can set up and manage Apple Watches for family members who don't have iPhones, such as school-age children or parents. This is possible if you are the family organizer or parent/guardian of the family sharing group.

To begin this process, the iPhone used for initial pairing must be within standard Bluetooth range of your Apple Watch. Additionally, family members must own a cellular-enabled Apple Watch SE or Apple

Watch Series 4 or later and be part of a

Family Sharing group. Available family

configurations vary by region. You can

use the Apple Watch app and Screen Time

on your iPhone to monitor and adjust

various settings, such as:

1. Communication boundaries

   and security measures

2. Screening schedule

3. School Time feature that

   limits certain Apple Watch

   features during school hours

4. Email and calendar settings

   for iCloud, Gmail, and other

   services

5. Restrict settings for explicit content, purchases, and privacy

You can also access activity, health, and location information for managed Apple Watches.

Note: When setting up an Apple Watch for a family member, interaction with the iPhone used for setup is limited.

To Set up your family's Apple Watch:

1. Make sure your family members are comfortable wearing their Apple

Watch, and adjust the band if
necessary.

2. Turn on your Apple Watch by
   pressing and holding the side
   button until you see the Apple logo.

3. Bring your iPhone close to your
   Apple Watch, wait until the pairing
   screen appears, then tap Next.

4. Or open the Apple Watch app, tap
   My Watches, select All Watches,
   then tap Add Watch.

5. Tap "Set for family" and tap "Next".

6. Position your iPhone so that your
   Apple Watch appears in the
   viewfinder to complete pairing.

7. Tap Set up Apple Watch and follow the onscreen instructions to complete setup.

To Manage your family's Apple Watch:

1. Open the Apple Watch app on your iPhone to manage your watch.
2. Tap My Watch, go to Family Watch, select your watch, then tap Done.
3. Under My Watch, explore the various managed Watch settings.

Note: Not all features available on personal Apple Watches are available on managed Watches.

Set Screen Time:

Use Screen Time to set up controls for your family's Apple Watch.

1. Open the Apple Watch app on your iPhone to manage your watch.

2. Tap My Watch, go to Family Watch, select your watch, then tap Done.

3. Tap Screen Time, tap Screen Time Settings, then tap Turn Screen Time On.

4. Configure options for content, communication security, screen-free time, and app/website restrictions.

5. Set a Screen Time passcode.

Alternatively, open the Settings app on your iPhone, go to Screen Time, select your family member's name under Family, turn on Screen Time, and configure settings accordingly.

Introducing Back to School on Apple Watch

School Time is a feature on the Apple Watch that is used to limit certain functions of the watch during school hours to encourage the wearer's focus.

Set class time:

1. Open the Apple Watch app on the iPhone you manage.

2. Tap My Watches, go to Family Watches, and select the appropriate watch.

3. Tap Done and select Class Hours.

4. Enable School Time and tap Edit Schedule.

5. Define specific days and times when Schooltime is enabled.

6. 6Add multiple schedules at different times throughout the day if needed.

End of school:

While School Time is active, family members can temporarily exit to check the activity ring or perform other tasks.

1. Tap the display or press and hold the Digital Crown.

2. Select "End" to temporarily end School Time.

If you finish School Time within the scheduled time, lower your wrist to see the School Time face again. For unscheduled times, School Time will remain inactive until the next scheduled start time or until you manually activate it in Control Center.

Unlock class time reports:

Receive reports on school time start times and stay up to date on family activities.

1. Open the Apple Watch app on the iPhone you manage.

2. Tap My Watch, access Family Watch, and select your watch.

3. Tap Done and go to Class Hours to view unlock reports for a specific day, time, or period.

4. On your Apple Watch, the report will appear under School Time in the Settings app.

Tips for activating class time:

Outside of scheduled hours, family members can manually enable class time as needed, such as after-school study groups.

1. Press the side button.

2. Tap the School Time button in Control Center to turn it on.

3. To exit, press and hold the Digital Crown and tap Exit. Class hours will resume based on your schedule or when manually enabled in the Control Center.

Listen To Music on Your Managed Apple Watch

If you're a member of a Family Sharing group with an Apple Music Family subscription, you can easily enjoy music on your managed girlfriend's Apple Watch as long as you have a Wi-Fi or cellular connection.

1. Open the Music app on your managed Apple Watch and access the Listen Now screen. This screen displays a personalized music selection based on your preferences. Plus, discover curated

playlists for kids and teens created by Apple Music editors.

2. To play music from your library, tap the Back button and choose one of the following options:

- Tap Radio to enjoy Apple Music Radio and genre stations.

- Tap Library to search for music stored directly on your Apple Watch.

- Tap Search to search for a specific artist, album, or play using typing (available only on supported models and language restrictions may apply), dictation, or doodle. Search the list.

Note: Doodle feature may not be available in all languages.

3. Use music controls in the Music and Now Playing apps to manage playback and make selections seamlessly.

View Family Activity and Health Reports

With your family's consent, you can access reports with detailed activity and health information.

Add your family health information and medical ID

To enter your family's health information or medical ID, follow these steps:

1. Open the Apple Watch app on your iPhone to manage your watch.

2. Tap My Watches, select Family Watch, and select the appropriate watch.

3. Tap Done, go to Health, and select Request health information for [name of family member].

4. Once you submit your health data request, a notification will be sent to your managed watch.

Once your family agrees to share their health information,

- Tap Health Details to enter or change information such as date of birth, height, weight, etc.

- Tap "Set Medical ID" to add emergency contacts, etc. When family members share this information through the Health app, their health details and medical ID can be viewed both on the iPhone that manages Apple Watch and on the watch itself.

- On iPhone: Open the Health app, go to Share,

select your family member's name, then tap Profile.

- On a managed Apple Watch: Open the Settings app and select Health.

Confirm family health information

If your family agrees to share their health information, you can access additional details about your family's activities, including information such as hearing, sun exposure, and heart rate.

1. Open the Health app on your iPhone and tap Share.

2. Select the family member's name listed under Shared with you.

3. Tap Health Categories and select a specific category to explore further.

APPLE WATCH BASICS

Integrated Application

Apple Watch comes with a number of important apps to improve your experience. These include:

- Activities

- Alarm

- App store

- audio books

- Blood Oxygen (available on Apple Watch Series 6, Apple Watch Series 7, Apple Watch

Series 8, and Apple Watch

Series 9 in select regions)

- Calculator

- Calendar

- Camera remote control

- Compass (available on Apple

  Watch SE and Apple Watch

  Series 5 and later)

- Contact address

- Cycle tracking

- ECG (electrocardiogram)

- Search for devices

- Find items

- Find people

- Pulse beat

- House

- Post

- Card

- Medicine

- Memoji

- Notice

- Mindfulness

- Music

- News (availability varies by region)

- Noise

- Currently running

- Phone

- Photograph

- Podcast

- Memory

- Remote controller

- Setting

- Connection

- Sleep

- Stock

- Stopwatch

- Timer

- Tips

- Voice memo

- Walkie-talkie (availability

  varies by region)

- Wallet

- Weather

- Train

- World clock

Expand your app collection with Apple Watch

Apple Watch comes with a variety of preinstalled apps for communication, health, fitness, and time management. Additionally, you can expand functionality by adding third-party apps directly from your iPhone or from the App Store on Apple Watch. All apps are conveniently organized on a unified home screen.

Note: Enable automatic download of companion iOS versions to ensure a seamless app experience. On your Apple Watch, go to Settings, tap App Store, and turn on automatic downloads. Please also enable automatic updates for the latest updates.

Purchase the app from the App Store on Apple Watch

1. Launch the App Store app on your Apple Watch.
2. Explore featured apps and curated collections using the Digital Crown.
3. Tap Collections to find more apps.

4. Tap Get to get the free app or tap the price shown to purchase.

5. For a specific app, tap the Search button in the top left and enter the app name (Scribbling and Dictation are available for supported models and languages). Or you can tap a specific category to see what's trending.

6. For compatible models of Scribble, swipe up from the bottom and select "Scribble".

Note: Data charges may apply when you use Apple Watch with cellular service. The available doodles vary by language.

I already have the app installed on my iPhone

If you prefer a more hands-on approach to installing apps, you can customize the process.

1. Open the Apple Watch app on your iPhone.

2. Go to My Watch and tap General to turn off automatic app installation.

3. Scroll down to Apps available on your watch.

4. Select Install next to the app you want to install on your Apple Watch.

Check The Time on Your Apple Watch

Apple Watch offers several convenient ways to check the time.

1. Wrist raise:

- Simply raise your wrist to see the time on your watch face, in the clock grid view, and in the top right corner of most apps.

2. Viewing time:

- Open the Settings app on your Apple Watch, tap Clock, and turn on Talk Time. To hear the time announced, press and hold the dial with two fingers.

- Optional: Enable Chime in Clock Settings to enable hourly chime. Under Sound, choose either bell or bird.

3. Tap time:

- Experience the sensation of a light tap on your wrist to discreetly read the time. Turn on Taptic Time in the Settings app on your Apple Watch, go to Clock, tap Taptic Time, turn on Taptic Time, and select the option you want.

Note: If Taptic Time is inactive, your Apple Watch may be set to announce the time audibly. To switch to Taptic Time, go to Settings > Clock and turn on Do Not Disturb Control under Call Duration.

4. Siri support:

- Easily find out the current time by raising your wrist and asking Siri, "What time is it?"

Choose the method that suits your preferences and make time management on your Apple Watch a personalized and accessible experience.

Use Control Center on Apple Watch

Control Center provides a convenient hub for managing various settings on your

Apple Watch. Easily check your battery, enable Do Not Disturb, select your focus, use the flashlight feature, enable airplane mode, enable cinema mode, and more.

Open and close Control Center:

- Open Control Center: Press the side button once.

- Close Control Center: With Control Center open, tilt your wrist or press the side button again.

To check the status of Control Center:

- Icons at the top of the Control Center show the

status of settings such as
mobile connectivity,
location usage, and active
features such as Airplane
mode and Do Not Disturb
mode.

- To view details, press the
  side button to open Control
  Center and tap the icon.

Control Center Customization:

- Reorder buttons: Press the side
  button to open Control Center,
  scroll down, tap Edit, and drag
  buttons to new positions. When
  finished, tap Done.

- Delete button: Press the side button to open Control Center, scroll down and tap Edit, then use the Delete button. When finished, tap Done.

- Restore deleted buttons: Open Control Center, tap Edit, and to restore deleted buttons. When finished, tap Done.

Airplane mode:

- Turn it on: Press the side button to open Control Center and tap the Airplane mode button.

- Use Siri: Say "Turn on airplane mode."

- Manage settings: Open Settings > Airplane mode to adjust Wi-Fi and Bluetooth behavior.

Flashlight function:

- Enable: Press the side button, open the control center and tap the flashlight button. Swipe left to switch between different modes.

- Adjust brightness: Rotate the Digital Crown up or down.

- To disable: Press the Digital Crown or Side button, or

swipe down from the top of the watch face.

Theater mode:

- Activation: Press the side button and tap the Cinema Mode button to confirm.

- Wake up Apple Watch: Tap the screen and press the Digital Crown or side button, or rotate the Digital Crown.

Disconnect from Wi-Fi:

- Temporarily disconnect: Press the side button, open Control Center, and tap the Wi-Fi button.

sleep mode:

- Enable: Press the side button and tap the "Do Not Disturb" button.

- Settings app: Open the Apple Watch app on your iPhone, go to My Watch > Sounds & Haptics, and turn on Do Not Disturb.

Ping your iPhone and find it accurately:

- Ping iPhone (Series 8 and earlier): Press the side button and tap Ping iPhone.

- Precise Search (Series 9):
  Press the side button and tap
  "Ping iPhone" to use the
  directions feature.

**Ping your Apple Watch from your
iPhone:**

- Setup: Open your iPhone
  settings, tap Control Center
  and add "Ping My Watch".
- Ping Apple Watch: In Control
  Center, swipe down from the
  top-right corner and tap Ping
  Apple Watch.

Stay in control of your Apple Watch
settings and easily access them from

Control Center to improve your overall
user experience.

Customize Apple Watch Display, Sound, And Haptic Settings

Adjust brightness and text:

1. Open the Settings app on your Apple Watch.
2. Go to "Display & Brightness".
3. Adjust brightness: tap the control or slider and use the digital crown.

4. Change font size: Tap "Text Size" and tap the font or rotate the Digital Crown.

5. Enable Bold Text: Enable bold text.

Alternatively, you can adjust these settings on your iPhone in the Apple Watch app under My Watch > Display & Brightness.

Adjust the sound:

1. Open the Settings app on your Apple Watch.

2. Access sound and haptics.

3. Change alarm volume: Tap the volume control or slider

and use the Digital Crown to
adjust.

Alternatively, you can adjust the volume
of your iPhone's alarm in Sounds &
Haptics in the Apple Watch app.

Adjust the haptic intensity:

1. Open the Settings app on your
   Apple Watch.
2. Tap "Sounds and Haptics".
3. Enable haptic alerts.
4. Select the haptic intensity
   from "Standard" or
   "Significant".

Alternatively, you can adjust these
settings on your iPhone in the Apple

Watch app under My Watch > Sounds & Haptics.

Turn digital crown haptics on or off:

1. Open the Settings app on your Apple Watch.
2. Go to Sounds and Haptics.
3. Turn crown haptics on or off.
4. Optionally, you can use the same steps to control the system's haptics.

Alternatively, you can manage her Digital Crown Haptics on your iPhone in My Watch > Sounds & Haptics in the Apple Watch app.

These adjustments let you customize your Apple Watch experience by adjusting display brightness, text size, sound, and haptic feedback to your liking.

Customize Your Apple Watch Notification Settings

Customize app notification settings:

1. Open the Apple Watch app on your iPhone.

2. Tap "My Watch" and select "Notifications".

3. Select an app (such as Messages) and tap Custom.

Select option:

- Allow notifications: Display notifications in Notification Center.

- Send to Notification Center: Send the notification to Notification Center without sound or display.

- Notifications Off: Disable app notifications.

- Customize notification grouping.

- Off: No grouping.

- Automatic: Group
  notifications based on app-
  specific information.

- By App: Group all app
  notifications.

Manage notifications directly on Apple Watch:

- Swipe left on your Apple
  Watch notifications.

- Tap the Details button to
  see the following options:

- Mute for 1 hour or Mute
  today: Notifications are
  temporarily muted.

- Add to Summary: Place
  future notifications in your
  iPhone's notification
  summary.
- Turn off time-sensitive:
  Prevents immediate
  delivery of time-sensitive
  notifications.
- Turn off: Disable app
  notifications.

Customize lock screen notifications:

1. Open the Settings app on your
   Apple Watch.
2. Tap "Notifications".
3. Configure lock screen options.

4. Show summary when locked:
   Show summary of
   notifications when locked.

5. Tap to see full notification: To
   see all notification details, you
   need to tap.

6. View notifications when your
   wrist is down: View
   notifications even when your
   wrist is down.

Customizing these settings creates a
customized notification experience on
your Apple Watch, allowing you to

manage your alerts and summaries the
way you want.

Manage Apple ID settings on Apple Watch

Edit personal data:

1. Open the Settings app on your Apple Watch.

2. Tap your name and select Personal Information.

3. Edit your name by tapping to select First Name, Middle Name, or Last Name.

4. Tap "Birthday" and enter a new date to change your birthday.

5. Subscribe or unsubscribe from announcements, recommendations, or the Apple News newsletter in your communication settings.

Apple ID password and security:

1. Open the Settings app on your Apple Watch.

2. Tap your name and select Sign-in & Security.

3. Manage your Apple ID password, email address, and phone number.

4. Tap Delete email address and select Delete email address to delete your verified email address.

5. Add an email address or phone number by tapping Add email or phone number and entering the information.

6. Tap "Change Password" and follow the onscreen instructions to change her Apple ID password.

7. Edit or add trusted phone numbers for two-factor authentication.

Sign in with Apple settings:

1. Open the Settings app on your Apple Watch.

2. Tap your name and select Sign in with Apple.

3. Manage Sign in with Apple settings for an app or website.

4. Select Stop using Apple ID to disconnect your Apple ID from the app.

5. Tap Forward to, select an address, and hide your email address.

Recovery key and subscription:

1. Open the Settings app on your Apple Watch.
2. Tap your name to:
3. Show recovery key status.
4. Manage your subscriptions and view costs, terms and options.
5. Cancel your subscription directly or resubscribe an expired subscription.

View and manage devices:

1. Open the Settings app on your Apple Watch. - Tap your name to:

2. Scroll down and tap a device to view its information.

3. If your device is not recognized, remove it from your account.

Use Apple Watch Shortcuts

In progress links:

1. Launch the Shortcuts app on your Apple Watch.

2. Select a shortcut from the list.

Add link complication:

1. Long press on the clock face and tap Edit.

2. Swipe left to go to Complications screen and select Complications.

3. Scroll to "Shortcuts" and select your shortcut.

Added more Apple Watch shortcuts:

1. Open the Shortcuts app on your iPhone.

2. Tap the "More" button in the top right corner of the shortcut.

3. On the Shortcuts screen, tap the Info button and turn on Show on Apple Watch.

Set Up Handwashing on Your Apple Watch

Enforce hand washing:

1. Launch the Settings app on your Apple Watch.
2. Select "Handwash" and turn on the handwash timer.

Please use handwash timer:

- Apple Watch detects when you start washing your hands and starts a 20-second timer.

- If you finish washing your hands before 20 seconds, a message will appear to remind you to finish.

Hand-washing reminder for family members:

1. To Enable handwashing reminders in your family's Apple Watch settings.

2. Go to Handwashing, enable handwashing timer, and

enable handwashing

reminders.

See hand washing report:

1. Access the Health app on your
   iPhone.

2. Go to Browse > More stats
   and tap Handwashing to see
   average handwashing time.

Connect your Apple Watch
to your Wi-Fi Network

Select your Wi-Fi network:

1. Press the side button to open the control center.

2. Press and hold the Wi-Fi button to select an available network.

3. Apple Watch is compatible with 802.11b/g/n 2.4GHz networks.

Enter Wi-Fi password:

1. If necessary, enter your password using your Apple Watch's keyboard or scribbling on the screen.

2. Use the Digital Crown to select uppercase or lowercase letters.

Alternatively, you can select a password from the list and tap Join.

Using a private network address:

1. Press the side button to open the control center.
2. Hold the Wi-Fi button and tap the connected network.
3. Disable private addresses if your network requires them.

Forgot network:

1. Press the side button to open the control center.

2. Press and hold the Wi-Fi
   button and select your
   network.
3. Tap "Forget this network" to
   remove it from your Apple
   Watch.

Connect your Apple Watch to your Bluetooth audio device

Connect Bluetooth headphones or speakers:

- Enabling audio playback on your Apple Watch via Bluetooth headphones or speakers is ideal for scenarios where you don't use your iPhone.

Pairing process:

- If you set up Air-Pods on your iPhone, just press Play and they work seamlessly with your Apple Watch.

- Follow the instructions on your Bluetooth headphones or speaker to enter discovery mode.

Bluetooth pairing:

1. Open the Settings app on your Apple Watch and access Bluetooth.

2. Tap the detected device in the list.

Alternatively, you can access Bluetooth settings using the Air-Play button in the Audiobooks, Music, Now Playing, or Podcasts app.

Audio output selection:

1. Press the side button to open the control center.

2. Tap the audio output icon and select your desired device.

Adjust headphone volume:

1. While using headphones, tap the Headphone Volume button in Control Center.

2. Check current volume via meter.

3. Tap the volume control or slider and use the Digital Crown to adjust.

Limit loud noise:

1. Manage headphone audio volume limits on Apple Watch.

2. Go to Settings > Sound &
   Haptics > Headphone Safety
   > Reduce Loud Sounds.
3. Enable and set desired decibel
   level.

Headphone volume monitoring:

1. While using headphones,
   open Control Center and tap
   the volume button on your
   headphones.
2. Check the meter to ensure
   safe audio levels.

**Receive headphone audio
notifications:**

- Apple Watch notifies you when headphone audio levels reach potentially harmful levels.
- To access details, go to Settings > Sound & Haptics > Headphone Safety.

- Alternatively, you can view notifications in the Health app on your iPhone under Browse > Hearing > Headphone Notifications.

Use Your Apple Watch Separately from Your Paired iPhone

For Apple Watch with cellular capabilities:

With mobile features and active plans, Apple Watch helps you stay connected even when your iPhone isn't nearby.

For all other Apple Watch models:

You can perform a variety of tasks without needing an iPhone or a Wi-Fi connection.

Functional on non-iPhone devices:

- play music

- Play podcasts

- Play audiobooks

- Record and play voice memos

- Use public transport cards and student cards

- Find people, devices and objects

- Use clock functions, world clock, alarm, timer, stopwatch

- View photos from synced albums

- Shop in-store with Apple Pay
- Access calendar events
- Track your activities and workouts
- Monitor your heart rate, edit your sleep schedule, measure blood oxygen levels, track your menstrual cycle, and practice conscious relaxation and breathing.
- Measure the noise level of your surroundings and headphones.

Advanced features with built-in GPS and altimeter:

- Apple Watch's integrated GPS provides accurate distance and speed information during outdoor workouts, even when your iPhone isn't paired.

- Built-in barometric altimeter improves accuracy during ascent and descent.

- Apple Watch SE, Apple Watch Series 6, and later

models include an always-on altimeter for real-time elevation updates.

Connect via Wi-Fi:

When connected to Wi-Fi, Apple Watch can perform multiple tasks independently, even when your iPhone is turned off.

- Get app from the App Store

- Send a message

- Make a call (requires Wi-Fi calling or FaceTime voice call within Wi-Fi range)

- Use walkie-talkie

- Stream music, podcasts, and audiobooks

- Add music

- Check weather conditions

- Track your inventory

- Control of smart home devices

- Use third-party apps that support Wi-Fi connectivity

Wireless technology:

Apple Watch uses Bluetooth® technology to connect to a paired iPhone and enjoy a variety of wireless features. The watch can independently configure Wi-Fi networks and connect to networks previously set up or accessed through a paired iPhone.

Set Up and Use Cellular Service on Apple Watch

Unlock Extensions:

With cellular capabilities and connected to the same cellular provider as your iPhone, Apple Watch lets you enjoy many features even when you're away from your iPhone or don't have Wi-Fi.

Note: Cell phone service availability may vary by region and carrier.

Enable Cellular Service:

You can activate your cellular service during initial setup or later by following these steps:

1. Open the Apple Watch app on your iPhone.
2. Tap "My Watch" and select "Cellular".
3. Follow the instructions to check your carrier's service plan and turn on cellular service on your Apple Watch.

Transfer an existing plan:

Use the following steps to transfer your existing cellular plan to another Apple Watch with cellular capabilities.

1. On your current Apple Watch, open the Apple Watch app on your iPhone.

2. Tap My Watch, go to Cellular, and tap the About button next to your cellular plan.

3. Select "Delete [provider name] plan" and confirm.

4. Contact your mobile phone provider if necessary.

5. Wear your new Apple Watch, go to My Watch, tap Cellular, and follow the instructions to turn on cellular.

Turn your phone on or off:

Control your cellular usage to save battery power and stay connected.

1. Press the side button to open Control Center.

2. Tap the Cellular button.

3. Turn your phone on or off.

Note: Using your phone for extended periods of time will drain your battery faster, and some apps may require an iPhone connection for updates.

Please check the signal strength:

Check your phone's signal strength using the following methods:

1. Use the Explorer watch face with green dots to indicate signal strength.

2. When you open Control Center, you'll see a green bar representing your phone's connection status.

3. Add cellular complications to your watch face.

Monitor your data usage:

Track mobile data usage.

1. Open Settings on your Apple Watch.

2. Tap Cellular and scroll down
   to see your data usage for the
   current period.

By following these steps, you can optimize
and manage your Apple Watch's cellular
service for a seamless experience.

SAFETY FEATURES INTEGRATED INTO THE APPLE WATCH

Apple Watch Emergency Safety Features

Apple Watch provides valuable security features in a variety of emergency situations.

Show important medical information:

Apple Watch has a Medical ID feature that you can access in case of an emergency. This ID will appear on your lock screen and give respondents access to important details such as your age, blood type, medical history, and allergies.

To access your medical ID:

1. Press and hold the side button until the slider appears.
2. Slide the Medical ID slider to the right.
3. Tap Done when finished.

Alternatively, you can access this feature by going to SOS > Medical ID from the Settings app on your Apple Watch.

Start emergency services on Apple Watch

To contact emergency services on your Apple Watch, use one of the following methods:

1. Enable Side Button:

    i.   Press and hold the side button until the slider appears.

    ii.   Drag the "Emergency call" slider to the right.

    iii.   Apple Watch dials emergency services based on your region (e.g. 911).

or

i.   Press and hold the side button until you hear a beep and the countdown begins.

ii. When the countdown ends, Apple Watch automatically contacts emergency services.

iii. To prevent automatic countdown, disable automatic dialing in Settings > SOS.

2. Voice Activation:

- Use Siri by saying "Hey Siri, call 911."

3. Activate Messaging:

i. Open the Messages app, tap
New Message, and select Add
Contact.

ii. Type 911 in the number field,
compose and send your
message.

4. Automatic Initiative:

- Fall Detection triggers a
call if immobility is
detected after a significant
fall.

- If a serious car accident
occurs, Apple Watch can
sound an alarm and send

an emergency call after 20
seconds.

Cancel an emergency call:

If an emergency call is placed in error, tap
the End Call button, then tap End Call to
confirm.

Update emergency address:

To ensure accurate location information
for emergency services, please update
your emergency address.

1. Open the Settings app on your
   iPhone.
2. Go to Phone > Wi-Fi Calling.

3. Tap Update Emergency
   Address and enter the
   relevant information.

Manage Fall Detection

If needed, enable fall detection on Apple Watch to connect to emergency services.

If your date of birth is 55 or older, fall detection is automatically turned on during the Apple Watch setup process. For users between the ages of 18 and 55, you can manually enable fall detection.

1. Open the Settings app on your Apple Watch.

2. Go to SOS > Fall Detection

    and enable fall detection.

or

On your iPhone, go to the Apple Watch

app, tap My Watch, go to Emergency SOS,

and turn on Fall Detection.

Note: Disabling wrist detection prevents

your Apple Watch from automatically

calling emergency services if it detects a

serious fall.

Select either 'Always on' to detect

falls continuously, or 'On during training

only' to enable fall detection only during

training sessions. For users between the

ages of 18 and 55 who set up a new Apple

Watch with watchOS 8.1 or later, fall detection during exercise will be enabled by default. If you're upgrading from a previous watchOS version, manually enable the feature only during workouts.

Note: Although fall detection increases safety, it does not detect all falls. As physical activity increases, fall detection is more likely to be triggered by violent movements that mimic falls.

Manage Crash Detection

Apple Watch Series 8, Apple Watch SE (2nd generation), or Apple Watch Series 9 has the ability to alert emergency services if it detects a serious car accident.

Enable or disable crash detection:

Crash detection is enabled by default. If you want to turn off Apple notifications and automatic emergency alerts after a serious car accident, follow these steps:

1. Open the Settings app on your Apple Watch.
2. Go to SOS > Incident Detection and turn off critical incident calls.

Note: It's important to note that Apple Watch can't detect all car accidents.

SIRI

Use Siri on Apple Watch:

Harness the power of Siri on Apple Watch to seamlessly perform tasks and receive information. Siri can be used for a variety of functions, including translating phrases, identifying songs with instant Shazam results, and providing concise excerpts from search results. Easily launch Siri to streamline tasks that typically require multiple steps.

Siri command example:

- "How do you say 'How are you?' in Chinese?"

- "I'm going to start a 30-minute outdoor run."
- "Please tell Kathleen it's almost over."
- "Open the sleep app."
- "Open settings."
- "What song is this?"
- "What causes rainbows?"
- "What's the latest on me?"
- "What should I ask?"

How to use Siri:

Initiate a Siri request in a variety of ways.

1. Raise your wrist to verbally communicate with your Apple Watch.

2. Say "Hey Siri" or just "Siri" followed by your request.

3. Press and hold the Digital Crown to launch Siri.

Additional tips:

- Adjust Siri response settings in the Settings app.

- Choose when Siri speaks your response (always on, controlled in silent mode, headphones only).

- Display subtitles and transcriptions for Siri requests.

- Use "Type to Siri" for text input.

- Adjust Siri's pause time for more comfortable interactions.

- Manage your Siri history by deleting saved interactions for privacy reasons.

Note: Siri functionality may vary by language and region. Siri on your Apple Watch requires an internet connection.

Enable Call Notifications with Siri on Apple Watch

Allows Siri to announce incoming calls and notifications, including messages from apps like Messages, through supported headphones. This functionality also extends to compatible third-party applications.

1. Launch the Settings app on your Apple Watch.

2. Select "Siri".

3. Enable the Call Announcement option.

When you receive a call, Siri identifies the caller and asks you if you want to accept or decline the call. Simply answer "Yes" if

you agree, or "No" if you refuse.

APPLE WATCH FACES SELECTIONS

Explore Watch Faces in The Apple Watch Face Gallery

Face Gallery within the Apple Watch app provides a handy overview of all available watch faces. This gallery makes it easy to explore, customize, and add faces to your collection right from the app.

Access to Face Gallery:

1. Launch the Apple Watch app on your iPhone.

2. Tap on the "Face Gallery" option at the bottom of the screen.

Please select facial features:

1. Tap a specific face in the face
    gallery.

2. Choose features such as color
    and style to further customize.

3. Watch the face above change
    in real time as you try
    different options.

**Incorporate complications into
your face gallery:**

1. Select a face in the face
    gallery.

2. Select the location of the
    complication (top left, top
    right, or bottom).

3. Swipe to explore additional features available at this location and choose the one that suits your preferences.

4. If you decide not to introduce complications at this point, move to the top of the list and tap Off.

Add new face:

1. Tap a face in the face gallery.

2. Customize your face by selecting the features and complications you want.

3. Tap Add.

The face you choose is seamlessly added to your collection and automatically becomes the current face on your Apple Watch.

Change The Watch Face on Your Apple Watch

Personalize your Apple Watch face by choosing a theme, customizing colors and features, and adding it to your collection. You can switch faces at any time to access the appropriate timekeeping tools or just for a change.

Use Face Gallery in the Apple Watch app:

1. Find available watch faces.

2. Customize and add to your collection.

Customize directly on Apple Watch:

1. Long press on the clock face.

2. Swipe and tap on the desired face.

Add complications to your watch face.

Enhance your watch faces by adding special features called complications. This may include stock prices, weather forecasts, and information from other installed apps.

procedure:

1. Long press on the display when the watch face is visible.

2. Tap Edit.

3. Swipe left to see complications.

4. Tap a complication to select it and use the Digital Crown to select a new complication.

Create and customize your watch face collection.

Create a personalized collection of custom faces containing variations of the same design.

procedure:

1. Touch and hold the display while the current watch face is displayed.

2. Swipe left and tap the New (+) button.

3. Browse and select the watch face you want to add.

Manage and delete watch faces

Easily organize your collection and remove unnecessary dials.

For Apple Watch:

- Touch and hold the screen, swipe to your face and tap Delete.

iPhone (Apple Watch app):

1. Open the app, tap "My Watch" and tap "Edit" in the "My Faces" section.

2. Tap "Delete" next to the watch face you want to delete.

Be forewarned:

Adjust the time displayed on your watch face without affecting your alarms or notifications.

procedure:

1. Open Settings on your Apple Watch.

2. Tap "Clock".

3. Tap +0 Min and turn the
   Digital Crown to advance the
   clock (up to 59 minutes).

APPLE FITNESS PLUS

Get Started with Apple Fitness+:

Discover the world of fitness with Apple Fitness+. With your subscription, you'll get access to a variety of workouts including HIIT, yoga, core, cycling, strength training, and more. Plus, immerse yourself in guided meditations that offer 5-, 10-, or 20-minute sessions to improve your overall well-being.

Use Apple Watch for advanced metrics:

Get the most out of your workouts by wearing your Apple Watch. As he exercises, important metrics like heart rate and calories burned are seamlessly sent to his iPhone, iPad, and Apple TV. After your workout, this data is synced to your daily activity log.

Note: Apple Fitness+ availability varies by country or region.

Sign up for Apple Fitness+:

1. Open the Fitness app on your iPhone, iPad, or Apple TV.
2. Tap Fitness+ on your iPhone, select the Free Trial button, and follow the onscreen instructions.

Workout and trainer selection:

1. When it's time to work out, go to your fitness app.

2. Select a workout type and select a specific workout and trainer.

3. Access detailed information about each workout, including playlists, music genres, subtitles, and required equipment. Enjoy a preview of your workout before you start.

4. Discover each Apple Fitness+ trainer's unique personality, music taste, and training style through their bios and workout lists.

Track your progress and metrics:

1. Monitor your progress on each fitness ring during your workout.

2. Track your heart rate and calorie burn with Apple Watch.

3. Statistics for each workout will be displayed on the screen. Some sessions have burn bars that show you how your metrics compare to other sessions that completed the same workout.

4. Tap the screen during your exercise to adjust the metrics displayed.

Start An Apple Fitness+ Workout or Meditation

Easily start working out or meditating with Apple Fitness+ on your iPhone or iPad. These sessions are tailored to suit all fitness levels and challenge you whether you're a beginner or looking to revisit your favorite routines. Once you start training, you can pause, resume, and play your session as needed.

Start a workout or meditation:

1. Open your fitness app. Tap Fitness+ on your iPhone.

2. Select your activity type above and choose a specific workout or

meditation. Alternatively, you can search for categories such as "Popular" or "Guest Instructor Series."

3. Additional actions:

   a. *Add to My Library:* Tap the "Add Workout" button.

   b. *Preview:* Tap "Preview".

   c. *Access your playlists:* If you're an Apple Music subscriber, tap Listen to Music to open your playlists.

4. Start the activity.

   a. Start the activity by tapping the corresponding button.

b. For treadmill workouts, select Run or Walk to get accurate metrics.

5. You can start activities even if you're not wearing your Apple Watch, but metrics won't be collected. Tap "Exercise without a watch" to start exercising.

6. To stream to an AirPlay 2.0 compatible device (like your TV or HomePod), tap the screen while exercising, select the AirPlay button, and choose your destination.

7. During training, the trainer will demonstrate exercise modifications

for different performance levels. We can also guide you through the changes.

8. Use your own body weight instead of dumbbells.

Pause and resume:

Easily pause or resume your workout or meditation from the device you're playing the workout on or your Apple Watch.

For Apple Watch:

- Pause: Press the side button and Digital Crown at the same time, or swipe and tap Pause.
- Resume: Pause or swipe repeatedly, then tap Resume.

For iPhone or iPad:

- Pause: Tap the screen and select "Pause".

- Resume: Tap the "Play" button.

End and review:

Finish your workout or meditation using your device or Apple Watch.

For Apple Watch:

- Swipe right and tap End, then tap End Workout.

- View your workout summary and tap Done to return to the Workout app.

For iPhone or iPad:

- Tap the "End" button and select "End Training".

- View a workout summary and choose options like Add to My Library, Share, choose a Cooldown Workout, or tap Done to return to Apple Fitness+.

Post-class summary:

You can revisit your workout summary in the Fitness app on your iPhone. Courses with a checkmark icon on their thumbnail indicate completed sessions.

Create A Custom Plan

1. Create a personal fitness plan that fits your schedule and goals.

2. Tap Create Plan to start a custom plan with Fitness+.

3. Customize your plan to suit your preferences and goals by choosing your training days, duration per day, and activity type (HIIT, yoga, strength training, meditation, etc.).

Please note that Apple Fitness+ may not be available in all countries or regions.

APPS DESIGNED FOR USE WITH APPLE WATCH

Activity: App To Track Daily Activity

Track your daily movement and fitness goals using the Activity app on Apple Watch. This app monitors your daily activities and challenges you to reach fitness milestones. Track your stance frequency, effort level, and exercise time, with three colorful rings representing your progress. The goal is to improve your health by minimizing your sitting time, increasing your physical activity, and completing each ring each day.

Fitness apps on your iPhone create activity records. After tracking your activity for at least 6 months, it provides daily trend data such as active calories, exercise time, standing time, standing time, walking distance, cardio fitness, and walking speed. For detailed insights, go to the Fitness app on your iPhone, tap Overview, scroll to Trends, and compare your performance to your average activity.

Siri integration:

On Apple Watch Series 9 with watchOS 10.2 or later, ask Siri and say phrases like "How far did I walk today?" (Availability varies by language and region).

Note: *Apple Watch is not a medical device. Please be aware of important safety information when using the Wellness App.*

First step:

After you set up your Apple Watch, follow these steps to set up the Activity app.

1. Open the Activity app on your Apple Watch.

2. Use the Digital Crown to read the movement, exercise, and stance instructions, then tap Start.

Progress confirmation:

You can always check your progress by accessing the Activity app on your Apple Watch. The app displays three rings representing:

- Red Movement Ring: Actively burn calories.
- Green Exercise Ring: A few minutes of vigorous activity.

- Blue Stand Ring: Stand and move for at least 1 minute per hour.

For wheelchair users, the blue stand ring changes to a rolling ring to represent a rolling process of at least 1 minute per hour.

Weekly Summary:

1. Open the Activity app on your Apple Watch.
2. Tap the Weekly Overview button to see a comprehensive overview of your daily average and weekly progress as you close the ring.

Change your goal:

Customize your activity goals based on your preferences.

1. Open the Activity app on your Apple Watch.
2. Tap the Weekly Summary button.
3. Rotate the Digital Crown to the bottom of the screen and tap Change Goal.
4. Adjust your goal using the minus or plus buttons and tap Next.
5. When finished, tap OK.

Tip: *To change a specific goal, e.g. a training goal, rotate the Digital Crown towards the goal and tap Change Goal.*

Weekly notifications:

Receive notifications every Monday about the previous week's achievements and adjust your goals based on your performance.

Activity history:

Check your activity history in the Fitness app on your iPhone.

1. Open the Fitness app on your iPhone.

2. Tap Overview and go to the Activities pane.

3. Tap the Calendar button and select a date.

Trend analysis:

See daily trend data in the Fitness app on your iPhone.

1. Open the Fitness app on your iPhone.

2. In the Trends section, tap More to see daily trends for various metrics.

Note: Up arrows indicate maintenance or improvement, and down arrows indicate a decline in the 90-day moving average.

Awards and achievements:

Earn awards for personal records, streaks, and milestones. Access from Apple Watch.

1. Open the Activity app on your Apple Watch.

2. Tap the Awards button to explore the different award categories.

You can also view your awards in the Fitness app on your iPhone.

Training and meditation history:

See your workout and meditation completion data in Apple Fitness+, the Workout app, or compatible third-party apps.

1. Open the Activity app on your Apple Watch.

2. Scroll to the bottom of the screen and tap to view a specific workout or meditation.

Activity Reminder:

Set reminders and track your goals.

1. Open the Settings app on your Apple Watch.

2. Tap Activity and set notifications.

3. Alternatively, open the Apple Watch app on your iPhone, tap My Watch, then tap Activity.

Pause daily coaching:

Follow these steps to turn off activity reminders.

1. Open the Settings app on your Apple Watch.

2. Tap Activities and turn off Daily Coaching.

3. Alternatively, open the Apple Watch app on your iPhone, tap My Watch, Activities, and turn off Daily Coaching.

Alarm: Set an Alarm

You can use the Alarm app on your Apple Watch to play a sound or activate vibrations at specific times.

Use Siri:

Type a command to Siri, such as "Set a repeating alarm for 6 a.m."

Steps to set an alarm on Apple Watch:

1. Open the Alarms app on your Apple Watch.

2. Tap the Add button.

3. Select AM or PM and use the digital crown to set hours or minutes. *(This step is not required if you are using the 24-hour format.)*

4. Turn the Digital Crown to make adjustments and tap the Review button.

5. Tap the switch to turn the alarm on or off. Alternatively, you can tap the alarm time and set repeat, label, and snooze options.

Tip: *To create a silent alarm that only vibrates, enable silent mode.*

Manage alarms:

Slumber:

When the alarm goes off, you can tap Snooze to delay the alarm for a few minutes. If you want to turn off the snooze function, do the following:

1. Open the Alarms app on your Apple Watch.

2. Tap each alarm in the list to disable the snooze function.

Delete:

To delete an alarm:

1. Open the Alarms app on your Apple Watch.

2. Tap an alarm in the list.

3. Scroll down and tap Delete.

Skip alarm:

If the alarm is part of your sleep schedule, you can skip it for just one night.

1. Open the Alarms app on your Apple Watch.

2. Tap the alarm under Alarms, then tap Skip Tonight.

Sync alarms between iPhone and Apple Watch:

Set an alarm on your iPhone and ensure syncing.

1. Open the Apple Watch app on your iPhone.
2. Tap My Watch, go to Clock, and turn on push notifications on your iPhone.

Apple Watch notifies you when your alarm goes off, so you can sleep or close it without a notification on your iPhone.

Bedside clock with alarm:

Set your Apple Watch as a bedside clock with an alarm.

1. Open the Settings app on your Apple Watch.

2. Go to General > Bedside Mode and enable Bedside Mode *(When Apple Watch is on the charger, this mode displays charging status, current time and date, and set alarm time).*

3. When in bedside mode, you can check the time by tapping or tapping the display.

4. If you set an alarm with an alarm clock app, Bedside mode will gently wake you up with a clear alarm sound.

5. When the alarm goes off, press the side button to turn off the alarm or press the Digital Crown to snooze for an additional 9 minutes.

Audiobooks: Enjoy Your Favorite Audiobooks

Enjoy your favorite audiobooks from Apple Books using the Audiobooks app on Apple Watch.

Play saved audiobooks:

1. Connect your Apple Watch to Bluetooth headphones or speakers, then launch the Audiobooks app.

2. On the Listen Now screen, use the Digital Crown to move through the video.

3. Tap the audiobook you want to start playing.

Stream audiobooks from your library:

When your Apple Watch is near your iPhone or connected to Wi-Fi (or cellular on compatible models), you can stream audiobooks from your library.

1. Open the Audiobooks app on your Apple Watch.

2. On the Listen Now screen, press the back button, go to your library, and tap the audiobook to start playing.

Play family audiobooks:

You can also enjoy audiobooks that Family Sharing members have purchased from Apple Books.

1. On the audiobook screen, tap "My Family."

2. Select the audiobook you want to play.

Siri commands for playback:

Use Siri to start playing audiobooks using voice commands.

"Play the audiobook 'The House in the Pines'."

Playback control options:

1. Adjust volume:

Rotate the Digital Crown to fine-tune the volume.

2. AirPlay device selection, chapter selection, speed adjustment:

Open the Audiobooks app on your Apple Watch and tap the More options button.

Select AirPlay device:

- Tap "AirPlay" and select the required device.

Please select chapter:

156

- Tap "Title".

Change playback speed:

- Tap the plus and minus buttons to
  select playback speeds such as
  0.75x, 1x, 1.25x, 1.5x, 1.75x, 2x, etc.

Blood Oxygen: Monitor Your Blood Oxygen Levels

Use the Blood Oxygen app on Apple
Watch Series 6 or later to measure the
amount of oxygen carried from your lungs
to your body by red blood cells and gain
insight into your overall health and well-
being. Please note that these

measurements are not intended for medical use.

Important information:

Blood oxygen measurement functionality will no longer be available on Apple Watch devices sold by Apple in the United States (indicated by part numbers ending in LW/A) starting January 18, 2024. For verification information, see the Apple Watch Identification Guide.

Requirements:

Please make sure the Blood Oxygen Level app is available in your country or region. Please update your iPhone Xs or later to the latest iOS version.

Update your Apple Watch (Series 6, Series 7, Series 8, or Apple Watch Series 9) to the latest watchOS version.

Note: The Blood Oxygen Level app is designed for users 18 years of age or older. Verify or set your age with your medical ID.

Blood Oxygen Monitoring Settings:

1. Open the Settings app on your Apple Watch.
2. Tap Blood Oxygen and turn on blood oxygen measurement.

Blood oxygen measurement:

The Blood Oxygen Level app takes measurements periodically throughout the day with background measurements enabled. It can also be measured on demand.

1. Open the Blood Oxygen app on your Apple Watch.

2. Place your arm on a stable surface with your wrist flat and the Apple Watch screen facing up.

3. Tap Start and hold still during the 15 second countdown.

4. Once completed, review the results and tap Done.

Note:

For best results, be careful not to touch the back of your Apple Watch to your skin. Wear it comfortably, allow your skin to breathe, and place it flush with the top of your wrist.

To disable background measurements in sleep focus or theater mode:

A bright red light is used to measure blood oxygen and can be more noticeable in dark environments. Disable the measurement if the light is disturbing.

1. Open the Settings app on your Apple Watch.

2. Tap Blood Oxygen Level and turn off Sleep Focus and Theater Mode.

Blood Oxygen History Check:

1. Open the Health app on your iPhone.

2. Go to Browse, tap Respiratory, and select Blood Oxygen.

Calculator: Perform Basic Arithmetic Calculations

Use the Calculator app on Apple Watch to perform basic arithmetic calculations, such as simple tip calculations and bill splitting.

Start Siri:

- Ask Siri math questions like "What is 73 x 9?" or "What is 18% of 225?"

Perform the calculation:

1. Open the Calculator app on your Apple Watch.

2. Tap the numbers and operators to get the results.

Split check and tip calculation:

1. Open the Calculator app on your Apple Watch.

2. Enter the total bill amount and tap "Tip".

3. Rotate the Digital Crown to select the tip percentage.

4. Tap People and enter the number of people you want to share your bill with using Digital Crown.

5. View the tip amount, total bill amount, and individual shares if the bill is split evenly.

Note: *Chip availability may vary by region.*

Important:

If you remove the Calculator app from your iPhone, it will also be removed from your Apple Watch.

Calendar: Manage Your Calendar

The Calendar app on Apple Watch helps you stay organized by showing you events scheduled for the past six weeks and the next two years. Here's how to check and update your calendar efficiently:

Enable Siri:

- Get quick information by issuing voice commands like "What's the next event?"

View calendar events:

1. Open the Calendar app on your Apple Watch, or tap a date or calendar event on your watch face.

2. Scroll through upcoming events using the Digital Crown.

3. Tap an event to see detailed information such as time, location, invitee status, and notes.

Pro Tip: *To return to the next event, tap the Back button in the top left corner.*

Change view settings:

1. Open the Calendar app on your Apple Watch.

2. Tap the More Options button and select a display toggle option.

- Next: View upcoming events for this week.

- List: Shows all events from the past 2 weeks to the next 2 years.

- Day, Week, or Month: Display events for the selected time period.

3. To move through the days, swipe left or right and tap the

current time to return to the present.

Moving between weeks and months:

For day or list views:

- Show current week: tap the Back button.

- View another week: swipe left or right.

- View events for a specific week: tap a date on the weekly calendar.

- Show current month: Tap the back button while showing this week.

- Show different months: Turn the Digital Crown.

- Select a week in the monthly calendar: Tap the week.

Adding, modifying, or deleting events:

- Create an event with specific details using Siri or the Calendar app.

- To delete or modify an event, tap the event and select the appropriate option.

- Instantly respond to invitations on your Apple Watch.

Get directions and customize notifications:

- Open the Calendar app and tap an event to access the address and get directions.

- Customize your Go Now notifications by adjusting the time interval in your iPhone's Calendar app.

Calendar settings:

To customize your calendar experience, change your notification settings and choose specific calendars to display on your Apple Watch.

1. Open the Apple Watch app on your iPhone.

2. Tap My Watch and go to Calendar.

3. Under Notifications or Calendar, select Custom.

The Apple Watch Calendar app makes it easy to manage your schedule and stay organized.

Camera Remote: Experience Photography

Improve your photography experience with Apple Watch's camera remote and timer features. You can take photos and videos remotely, so you can capture the perfect shot without any hassle. Here's how to get the most out of these features.

Activate Siri:

- Activate your camera remotely by simply saying "Take a photo."

Take a picture:

1. Open the Camera Remote app on your Apple Watch.

2. Frame your shot by positioning your iPhone with your Apple Watch as your viewfinder.

3. Tap the button area to adjust exposure and rotate the digital crown to zoom in.

4. Tap the shutter button to take a photo.

5. Check your photos on your Apple Watch and find them in the Photos app on your iPhone.

Record the video:

For watchOS 10 and above:

1. Open the Camera Remote app on your Apple Watch.

2. Frame the video you recorded with your Apple Watch.

3. Use the Digital Crown to zoom in.

4. Long press the shutter button to start recording.

5. Release the shutter button to stop recording.

Recording review:

After you take a photo or video, you can review the recording on your Apple Watch using the following actions:

- View photos: Tap the thumbnail in the bottom left.
- Move between photos: swipe left or right.
- Zoom in: Rotate the digital crown.
- Pan the zoomed photo: Drag on the screen.

- Fill the screen: Double-tap the photo.

- Show/hide close button and number of shots: tap the screen.

Once the confirmation is complete, tap Close.

Adjust camera settings:

1. Open the Camera Remote app on your Apple Watch.

2. Tap the More Options button to configure additional settings.

   - Timer (3 seconds delay on or off)

   - Camera (front or rear)

- Flash (auto, on or off)

- Live Photo (automatic, on or off)

Note: Make sure your Apple Watch is within Bluetooth range (approximately 10 meters) from your iPhone for smooth remote control of your camera. Easily take beautiful photos and videos with Apple Watch.

Electrocardiogram: Recording an Electrocardiogram (ECG)

If you have an Apple Watch Series 4 or newer model, you can use the ECG app to take an electrocardiogram and gain valuable insight into your heart's electrical activity. To record an ECG, follow these steps:

1. **Please check compatibility:**

   - Make sure you're using Apple Watch Series 4 or later.

   - Update your iPhone Xs or later to the latest iOS version.

   - Make sure your Apple Watch has the latest watchOS version installed.

2. **Set ECG:**

   - Open the Health app on your iPhone.

- Follow the on-screen

  instructions to set up the ECG.

- If you don't see the prompt,

  tap Browse, go to Heart, and

  select Electrocardiogram

  (ECG).

3. Start ECG on Apple Watch:

- Open the ECG app on your

  Apple Watch.

- Place your arms on a stable

  surface such as a table or your

  lap.

4. Recording:

- Place your finger on the

  digital crown from your other

  hand on the watch.

- Allows Apple Watch to record his ECG without pressing his Digital Crown.
- Wait until the recording is complete.

5. Post-recording actions:

- After enrollment, you will be assigned a class.
- Tap Add Symptom and select all relevant symptoms.
- Save the symptom and tap Done.

6. Show results:

- To see detailed results, open the Health app on your iPhone.

- Tap Browse, go to Heart, and select Electrocardiogram (ECG).

Important considerations:

- ECG app is not available on Apple Watch SE.
- Check availability in your area.
- For accurate readings, make sure your Apple Watch is dry before recording, especially after activities like swimming or sweating profusely.

- ECG function is designed for temperatures between 32° and 95° F (0° and 35° C).

By following these steps, you can easily record your ECG with your Apple Watch and gain valuable insight into your heart health.

Find App: Find And Connect with Friends

The Find People app on Apple Watch makes it easy to find and connect with friends and family who share your location. To get the most out of this feature, please follow these steps:

Add friend:

1. Open the Find People app on your Apple Watch.
2. Scroll down and tap Share My Location.
3. Select friends using dictation, contacts, or keyboard.
4. Select your email address or phone number.
5. Set the location sharing period to 1 hour, until the end of the day, or indefinitely.

Your friends will receive notifications about your shared location. They can retaliate by telling you, their location. Once mutually agreed, you can easily track your location using the Find My app on your iPhone, iPad, or Mac, or the Find People app on your Apple Watch.

To stop sharing your location with a friend, tap your friend's name on the Find People screen and select Stop Sharing. For more comprehensive actions, go to the Settings app on your Apple Watch, go to Privacy & Security > Location Services, and turn off Location Sharing.

Find a friend:

1. Open the Find People app on your Apple Watch.

2. View a list of your friends and their approximate location and distance.

3. Rotate the digital crown to see more friends.

4. Tap a friend to see their exact location and approximate address on the map.

5. Use Siri to issue voice commands such as "Where's Julie?"

Notification of departure or arrival:

1. Open the Find People app on your Apple Watch.

2. Tap your friend, scroll down and select "Notify [friend's name]."

3. Enable Notify [friend's name] and choose to notify them when you leave or arrive at your friend's location.

Receive notifications:

1. Open the Find People app on your Apple Watch.

2. Tap your friend, scroll down, and select Notifications.

3. Enable notifications and choose to receive notifications when friends leave or arrive at your location.

Stay connected and know where your friends are with these simple steps using Apple Watch.

Navigation and communication on Apple Watch

Use Apple Watch to get hassle-free directions and instantly communicate with friends using the Find People app.

Direction:

1. Open the Find People app on your Apple Watch.
2. Select your friend, then scroll down and tap Routes to launch the Maps app.

3. Follow Routes to get step-by-step directions from your current location to your friend's exact location.

Please contact a friend:

1. Open the Find People app on your Apple Watch.

2. Select your friend, then scroll down and tap Contacts.

3. Select an email address or phone number to start communicating immediately.

With these simple steps, you can easily stay connected and keep in touch with friends using your Apple Watch.

Heart Rate: Monitor Your Heart Rate

Checking your heart rate is a valuable way to assess your body's health. Apple Watch offers several options for tracking your heart rate whether you're exercising, breathing exercises, or any other time.

Voice activation with Siri:

- For Apple Watch Series 9 with watchOS 10.2 or later, use commands like "What is my heart rate?" or "What is your average heart rate while walking?" through Siri. (Availability varies by language and region.)

Note:

Water and sweat can affect accuracy, so make sure both your wrist and Apple Watch are clean and dry to get accurate readings.

Check your heart rate:

1. Open the Heart Rate app on your Apple Watch.

2. Instantly display and continuously monitor your current heart rate while wearing the watch.

Visualize heart rate data:

1. Open the Heart Rate app on your Apple Watch.

2. Rotate the digital crown to see your heart rate range, resting speed, or walking average for a comprehensive overview of your heart rate throughout the day.

3. For a longer time period, go to the Health app on your iPhone, go to Browse, tap Heart, and select the time period (hours, days, weeks, months, or years).

Enable heart rate data:

Enable heart rate monitoring by default for heart rate apps, workout sessions, breathing sessions and reflection sessions. If the feature is disabled, follow these steps to re-enable it.

1. Open the Settings app on your Apple Watch.
2. Go to Privacy & Security > Health.
3. Tap "Heart Rate" and turn on "Heart Rate".

- Alternatively, you can go to the Apple Watch app on your iPhone, tap My Watch, go to Privacy, and turn on Heart Rate.

Note:

For optimal functionality, keep the back of Apple Watch in contact with your skin to ensure a comfortable fit that allows

the sensors to work effectively.

Monitor your heart health with Apple Watch

Apple Watch monitors your heart health and provides timely notifications if any abnormalities are detected. This includes alerts if your heart rate falls above or below certain thresholds during periods of inactivity. Additionally, Apple Watch will alert you if it detects irregular heart rhythms that indicate atrial fibrillation (AFib). This will help you better understand and track if you have already been diagnosed with atrial fibrillation.

Enable high or low heart rate notifications:

1. Open the Settings app on your Apple Watch.

2. Tap "Heart".

3. Select "High Heart Rate Notification" or "Low Heart Rate Notification" and set the desired heart rate threshold.

4. Alternatively, you can use the Apple Watch app on your iPhone, tap My Watch, go to Heart, and set high or low heart rate thresholds.

Irregular heart rhythm notification

1. Open the Apple Watch app on your iPhone.

2. Go to My Watch, tap Heart, and select Set irregular rhythm alert under Health.

3. Follow the onscreen instructions in the Health app to complete setup.

AFib history display (availability varies):

1. If you've been diagnosed with atrial fibrillation, open the Health app on your iPhone.

2. Tap Browse, go to Hearts, then scroll down to Do More with Your Health.

3. In AFib History, tap Setup and follow the onscreen instructions.

4. To view your AF history, open the Health app, tap Browse, go to Heart, and select AF History.

Low aerobic fitness notification:

1. Open the Settings app on your Apple Watch.

2. Tap "Heart".

3. Select and enable cardio fitness notifications.

4. Alternatively, you can use the Apple Watch app on your iPhone, tap My Watch, go to Heart, and turn on Cardio Fitness Notifications.

Check out our cardio fitness measurements:

- Explore the Cardio Fitness section of the Health app to view your measurements and corresponding ranges (low, below average, above average, or high).

- Tap "See all cardio fitness levels" to see comprehensive information. Stay on top of your heart health and receive personalized notifications on Apple Watch to stay alert and proactive.

Home: Manage Your Smart Home

Turn your Apple Watch into a central hub for easily controlling HomeKit-enabled devices through the Home app. From lights and locks to smart TVs and thermostats, the Home app provides a safe and convenient way to manage a variety of accessories right from your wrist. You can also seamlessly access intercom messages and real-time video streams from HomeKit Secure Video cameras on supported devices.

The first time you open the Home app on your iPhone, a setup wizard will appear to guide you through creating a home. Define rooms, add HomeKit-enabled accessories, and create scenes to personalize your smart home experience. Accessories, scenes, and rooms set up on your iPhone integrate seamlessly with your Apple Watch.

Siri voice commands:

- Get quick, hands-free control with Siri voice commands like "turn off office lights."

Monitor your home:

1. **Open the Home app and access the various sections.**

   - Camera: Displays up to 4 camera video feeds. Tap here to view the live stream. - Categories: Rooms are divided into categories such as light, security, climate, speakers, and water.

- Related accessories: Display scenes and accessories based on the current context.

2. Smart Control Actions:

- Turn accessories on or off: Tap an accessory or use your Apple Watch as a home button on a compatible lock.

- Adjust settings: Tap the More options button on the accessory and go back using the Close button. - Control your favorite accessories, scenes, or room-specific accessories: Access your favorites, scenes, or specific

rooms to make quick
adjustments.

3. Show camera stream:

- Tap the camera to access the
  video stream. If you have
  more than 4 cameras, use the
  "+" button to see all options.

4. Run scene:

- Open the Home app on your
  Apple Watch and tap the
  scene you want to start.

Switching between houses:

If you have multiple homes set up, you
can easily switch between them on your
Apple Watch.

1. Open the Home app.

2. Double-tap the Back button.

3. Select the desired home.

Turn your Apple Watch into a powerful smart home controller that seamlessly manages connected devices and improves your home automation experience.

Memoji: Express Yourself with Memoji

Unleash your creativity and personalize your virtual identity with the Memoji app on Apple Watch. Choose skin tone, hairstyle, facial features, and more to create a unique Memoji that reflects your personality. Immerse yourself in the world of expression by designing multiple Memoji to suit different moods.

Create Memoji:

1. Open the Memoji app on your Apple Watch.

2. If this is your first time, tap Get Started. If you've already created a Memoji, scroll up and tap Add Memoji to design a new Memoji.

3. Tap each feature and use the Digital Crown to select your preferences and bring your Memoji to life with details like hairstyles and glasses.

4. Click the check button to add Memoji to your collection.

5. The Memoji you create can be converted into Memoji stickers for messages.

Edit and more:

Open the Memoji app on your Apple Watch and tap Memoji to explore your options.

- Edit Memoji: Use the Digital Crown to adjust features like eyes and hats and choose variations.

- Create a Memoji watch face: Scroll down and tap Create Watch Face to find your new Memoji watch face. It will be added to your watch face collection in the Apple Watch app on your iPhone.

- Duplicate Memoji: Scroll down and tap Duplicate to duplicate the Memoji.

- Delete Memoji: To delete a Memoji, scroll down and tap Delete.

Design, edit, and customize Memoji directly from your Apple Watch, letting your imagination run wild and adding uniqueness to your digital expression.

Messages: Messaging Made Easy

The Messages app on Apple Watch makes it easy to compose and send messages. You can use a variety of communication options, including text, images, emojis, Memoji stickers, audio clips, and even Apple Pay transactions. Here's a comprehensive guide to improve your messaging experience.

Compose a message on your Apple Watch:

1. Open the Messages app on your Apple Watch.
2. Tap the New Message button.

3. Select a contact from recent conversations or explore contact options.

4. Tap Compose Message.

Compose a text message:

1. After composing your message, tap the Compose Message field.

2. Enter text using QWERTY and QuickPath keyboards or Scribble.

3. You can use your iPhone to insert emojis, dictate text, and type text.

4. Get creative with predictive text or tap to select words.

send a message:

1. Open the Messages app on your Apple Watch.

2. Touch and hold the message bubble, then tap Unsend.

Edit the sent message:

1. Open the Messages app on your Apple Watch.

2. Select the conversation that contains the message you want to edit.

3. Touch and hold the message bubble, then tap Edit.

Send a smart reply, Memoji sticker, sticker, GIF, or audio clip:

Compose a message without typing:

- Send smart replies.

- Share Memoji stickers.

- Send a sticker or GIF.

- Share your location.

- Send audio clips.

Use Apple Cash:

1. Tap the app icon during a conversation.

2. Tap the "Apple Cash" button.

3. Enter the amount and tap "Send" or "Request".

4. Double click the side button to send a message.

Send sketches from Apple Watch:

1. Submit your sketch using Digital Touch.

2. Tap the app icon and tap the digital touch button.

3. Draw on the screen, choose a color and tap send.

Represented with digital touch:

1. Send a touch, a kiss, or a heartbeat.

2. Tap the app button, then tap the digital touch button.

3. Use gestures to send a touch, a kiss, a heartbeat, a heartbreak, or a fireball.

Enhance your messaging experience with rich features in the Messages app on Apple Watch, providing a seamless and expressive way to connect with friends and family.

Make FaceTime voice calls easier with Messages on Apple Watch

WatchOS 10 makes it easy to start group FaceTime audio calls using the Messages app on Apple Watch.

Start a group FaceTime audio call from a Messages conversation:

1. Open the Messages app on your Apple Watch.

2. Start a new message or access an existing conversation.

3. Scroll down and tap FaceTime Audio to start the call.

4. To add more participants, tap the More options button, select Add user and select a contact, or tap 2 active users and select Tap Add and select a contact.

Receive FaceTime audio calls:

When you receive a FaceTime voice call, you have several options for answering it.

Receive a call:

- Just tap the reply button.

Reject the call:

- To decline, tap the "End Call" button.

Reply by text message:

- Tap the More options button and select a canned answer. Or you can tap Custom to compose and send your message.

Add another person to the call after answering:

- If necessary, tap 2 people active, tap Add, and select contacts.

Alternatively, you can tap Add User and select a contact.

Watch recorded video messages:

- If you miss a FaceTime call, callers can leave a video message. To watch, tap the notification when you get it, or visit the conversation later in Messages and tap the video.

Tips: *Seamlessly manage FaceTime voice calls on your Apple Watch and improve your communication experience right from the Messages app.*

Seamlessly share your location in Messages on Apple Watch

You can let others know where you are by sharing your location in iMessage conversations in the Messages app.

Enable location sharing:

1. Open the Settings app on your Apple Watch.

2. Tap "Privacy & Security" and select "Location Services."

3. Tap Share My Location and make sure the option is turned on.

Alternatively, adjust the following settings on your paired iPhone:

1. Go to Settings > Privacy & Security > Location Services > Location Sharing.

2. Under Location Services, tap Messages and select Settings.

Easily share and update your location:

1. Open the Messages app on your Apple Watch.

2. Start a new message or open an existing conversation.

3. Tap the app button and select the "Search" button.

4. Choose whether to share your live location, update in real time, or share your static location.

   - *To share your live location:* Tap "Share".

- *To share static location:* Tap the Pin button, then tap Send Pin.

5. Set the period for sharing location information.

   - *Select Unlimited to share continuously until you manually stop it.*

6. Tap Send to send your message.

   - *To see your location, the recipient taps the message to open the Maps app.*

Stop sharing your location:

1. Open the Messages app on your Apple Watch.

2. Access the conversation and tap the message that includes your shared location.

3. Tap Stop Sharing.

Alternatively, open the Find People app, select the person, scroll down, and tap Stop Sharing.

Request someone else's location:

1. Open the Messages app on your Apple Watch.

2. Start a new message or open a conversation.

3. Tap the app button, select the Explore button, and select Request.

4. Tap Send to send your request.

After receiving the request, the recipient can share their location by tapping "Share".

Note: *Sharing your location in Messages may not be available in all regions.*

Music: Enjoy Music with Apple Watch

The Music app lets you seamlessly select and play music on your Apple Watch. Whether you want to access music stored locally, manage music on your iPhone, or stream as an Apple Music subscriber, your options are just a tap away.

Easy commands using Siri:

Use Siri by saying a command like this:

- "Please play 'Party Girls' by Victoria Monet."
- "Play your workout playlist."
- "Play Apple Music Country."
- "Please play more like this."

Start playing music:

After connecting your Apple Watch to Bluetooth headphones or speakers, open the Music app and follow these steps.

- Play music on Apple Watch: Scroll through the Listen Now screen and tap an album, playlist, or category.

- Control music from your library:
  Access your library from the Listen
  Now screen and tap to select a
  category, such as playlists, albums,
  downloaded, or recently added
  categories.

- Request music from Apple Music
  (registration required): Raise your
  wrist to request an artist, album,
  song, genre, or part of a lyric.

Music customized for you:

As an Apple Music subscriber, discover
music curated just for you:

1. Open the Music app on your Apple
   Watch.

2. Scroll down to find your recently added music and customized playlists based on your preferences.

3. Select a category, tap an album or playlist, and click the "Play" button.

Queue management:

Easily navigate your queue and upcoming songs.

1. Open the Music app on your Apple Watch.

2. Play an album or playlist, tap the More Options button, and select Play Next.

3. To play a specific song in your queue, tap on it.

Shuffle or repeat:

Customize your music experience with shuffle and repeat options.

- Tap the "More options" button on the playback screen, go to "Play next" and tap the "Shuffle" or "Repeat" button.
- To repeat a song, double tap the repeat button.
- Shuffle your library: On the Now Playing screen, tap Back, go to Library, select Artist, Album, or Song, then tap Shuffle All To do.

Streaming to other devices:

Extend your music experience beyond your Apple Watch. On the Now Playing screen, tap the More options button.

- Connect to a Bluetooth device: Tap AirPlay and select your device.
- Connect to an AirPlay device: Tap AirPlay, tap Control other speakers and TV, select your device, and choose your music.

Quick access to Now Playing:

You will immediately return to the Now Playing screen.

- On the Music app screen, tap the Now Playing button in the top right corner.

- On your watch face, with the Digital Crown facing up, tap the song currently playing in your Smart Stack, or click the Music button at the top.

Turn on the radio on your Apple Watch

Discover the diverse world of radio right from the Music app on Apple Watch with Apple Music 1, Apple Music Hits, and Apple Music Country. With a variety of genres, exclusive interviews, and carefully selected stations, you can enjoy a variety of music experiences without a subscription.

Listen to Apple Music Radio:

1. Make sure your Apple Watch is near your iPhone and connected to Wi-Fi or a cellular network (for cellular-enabled models).

2. Open the Music app on your Apple Watch.

3. Go to the Listen Now screen, tap Back, select Radio, then choose Apple Music 1, Apple Music Hits, or Apple Music Country.

Explore channels of your chosen genre:

1. Open the Music app on your Apple Watch.

2. On the Listen Now screen, tap Back, select Radio, and use the Digital Crown to scroll through our expertly crafted stations and genres.

3. Tap a genre to view its stations, then select the station you want to start playing.

Consider wireless options:

Discover additional features while listening to radio stations:

1. Open the Music app on your Apple Watch.

2. Tap Radio, select a station, then tap the More Options button.

3. Options include viewing upcoming songs, adding music to your library or playlist, sharing the song, setting preferences, and navigating to the Artist or Album screen.

Listen to the broadcast:

1. Activate Siri by saying a command like "Play Wild 94.9" or "Turn on ESPN Radio."

2. Specify the station, by station name, call sign, frequency or nickname.

3. Note: Radio shows do not require an Apple Music subscription.

Availability may vary by country or region.

News: Get the Latest News on Apple Watch

The News app on Apple Watch lets you stay up to date on the latest happenings with a customized selection of articles based on your interests.

Note: *News app availability is subject to country and regional restrictions.*

Search for messages:

1. Open the News app on your Apple Watch.

2. Tap the Add Message feature on your watch face.

3. Access the Messages widget on the Siri watch face.

4. Respond to news notifications.

Read the news:

1. Open the News app on your Apple Watch.

2. Use the Digital Crown to navigate through the stories list.

3. Tap a specific story to expand it.

4. To save the story to your iPhone, iPad, or Mac for later reading, scroll to the bottom of the story and tap the Bookmark button.

5. Access your saved stories later on your iPhone, iPad, or Mac.

     i. iPhone: Open News, tap Follow, select Saved Stories, then tap a story.

     ii. iPad: Open News, tap Saved Stories in the sidebar, then tap a story.

     iii. Mac: Open News, click Saved Stories in the sidebar, then click a story.

Share the news:

1. Open the News app on your Apple Watch.

2. Scroll to and tap the story you want.

3. Scroll down and tap the Share button and select a sharing option.

Story navigation:

1. Open the News app on your Apple Watch.

2. Scroll up or down to read the story, then tap Read More.

Open news alerts on iPhone:

1. Open the News app on your Apple Watch.

2. Start your iPhone and open App Switcher.

- On iPhone with Face ID, swipe up from the bottom to pause.

- On iPhones with a home button, double-click the home button.

3. Tap the button shown below to open News.

Noise: Monitor And Measure Environmental Noise Levels

The Noise app on Apple Watch uses your device's microphone and exposure time to measure ambient noise levels. When decibel levels reach levels that can affect your hearing, Apple Watch alerts you with a simple tap.

Note:

The Noise app uses your microphone only to sample and measure ambient noise levels. For this purpose, Apple Watch does not record or store sound.

Noise app setup:

1. Open the Noise app on your Apple Watch.

2. Tap Enable to enable monitoring.

3. To measure environmental noise in the future, visit the Noise app or use the Noise complication.

Receive noise alerts:

1. Open the Settings app on your Apple Watch.

2. Go to Noise > Noise Alert and select your preferred settings.

3. Alternatively, you can adjust your notification settings in the Apple Watch app on your iPhone by going to My Watch > Sound > Sound Threshold.

Disable noise measurement:

1. Open the Settings app on your Apple Watch.

2. Go to Noise > Ambient Sound Measurement and turn off Noise Measurement.

3. Alternatively, you can turn off ambient sound measurement by going to My Watch in the Apple Watch app on your iPhone and tapping Noise.

Tracking environmental noise pollution:

When your Apple Watch is paired with your iPhone and the Noise app is set up (requires watchOS 6 or later), your Apple Watch automatically sends ambient noise levels to the Health app on your iPhone.

Noise notification details:

Receive notifications from your Apple Watch on your iPhone when ambient noise reaches levels that can affect your hearing. To access notification details:

1. Open the Health app on your iPhone.
2. Tap "Summary" at the bottom left.
3. Select Sound Notifications at the top of the screen.
4. Tap Show more data to view detailed information.

Past ambient noise exposure:

Monitor your environmental noise exposure over time using the Health app on your iPhone.

1. Open the Health app.

2. Tap "Browse" in the bottom right corner and select "Listen."

3. Select Ambient Noise Level.

Options for analyzing noise pollution:

Displays exposure values over time:

- Tap the tab at the top of the screen. (The decibel value is used for measurement.)

Noise level classification:

- Tap the Info button to learn more about the different noise level classifications.

Adjust chart period:

- Swipe left or right on the graph to change the time period displayed.

Specific moment details:

- Long press on the chart and drag to move selection and view details.

Average exposure information:

- Tap Show detailed data and select Daily average to get detailed insights.

Visual representation of average exposure:

- Tap "Exposure" below the image.

Upper and lower range information:

- Tap "Show more data" and select "Range" to display the top and bottom panes.

Now Playing: Play and Enjoy Seamless Audio Controls

Now Playing lets you easily manage audio playback on your Apple Watch, iPhone, and a variety of other devices.

Currently open and running:

4. Launch the Now Playing app on your Apple Watch.

5. Tap the playing complication if it's added to your watch face.

6. When you approach a HomePod that is playing, it will automatically open and allow you to control playback.

Control audio with iPhone:

4. Open Music, Podcasts, or Books on your iPhone and start playing a song, podcast, or audiobook.

5. Access Now Playing on your Apple Watch for play, pause, and other controls.

6. Adjust the volume using the Digital Crown.

Now playable on various devices:

1. Open the Now Playing app on your Apple Watch.

2. If multiple devices are available (Apple Watch, iPhone, HomePod,

etc.), device icons will appear in the top right corner.

3. Tap Back to display the device list and select a device to control audio playback.

Play audio on iPhone:

1. Open the Now Playing app on your Apple Watch.

2. Tap Back and scroll to select iPhone.

3. Launch an audio app (audiobooks, music, podcasts) on your iPhone and select the audio file you want to play.

4. Sound will play through your iPhone's speakers or paired audio device.

Change or add AirPlay devices:

1. Open the Now Playing app on your Apple Watch.

2. On the Now Playing screen, tap More options.

4. Tap AirPlay and select and add your device.

5. To stop playing on a device, tap that device.

Find nearby suggestions for HomePod:

With watchOS 10.2, music and podcast suggestions appear in the Smart Stack widget when you're near a HomePod that isn't playing. Use the Digital Crown to scroll up to see suggestions, then tap to play on HomePod.

Phone: Easily Make Calls with Apple Watch

Enjoy the convenience of making calls on your Apple Watch with seamless voice commands from Siri.

Voice command:

- "Call Max"

- "Please dial 555 555 2949"

- "Call Pete's FaceTime Audio"

Make a call:

1. Open the Phone app on your Apple Watch.

2. Tap Contacts and scroll the Digital Crown.

3. Select the desired contact and tap the phone icon.

4. Tap FaceTime Audio or select a phone number to start a FaceTime audio call.

5. Adjust the call volume using the Digital Crown.

Additional tips:

- To call a current contact, tap Recent in your iPhone's Phone app, and tap Favorites.

- For group FaceTime calls (available in watchOS 10), follow similar steps and add participants using the More options button.

Make a Wi-Fi call:

1. Use Wi-Fi calling if your carrier supports it. Make sure Wi-Fi calling is enabled on your iPhone.

2. On your iPhone, go to Settings > Phone and turn on Wi-Fi calling.

3. Open the Phone app on your Apple Watch, select a contact, and tap the Call button.

Display call information:

- Monitor call information on your Apple Watch via the Phone app while you talk on your iPhone.
- Easily end calls directly from your Apple Watch. This is especially useful if you are using headphones or a headset.

Photos: Explore Your Photos and Memories

The Photos app lets you easily navigate through your precious memories and photos on your Apple Watch, and you can even view them on the watch face.

View photo:

1. Open the Photos app on your Apple Watch.

2. Find memories, featured photos, or synced albums.

3. Tap the photo to view it.

4. Swipe left or right to see more photos.

5. Use the Digital Crown to zoom or drag to pan.

6. Double tap to view the entire screen or view the entire image.

7. Zoom out to view the entire photo album.

Show reminders on your watch face:

Relive your memories not only with the Photos app, but also with Siri and photo watch faces.

- Select the Siri watch face and tap Reminders.

- On your photo face, open the Apple Watch app on your iPhone, go to your Face Gallery, select your photo face, and choose Dynamic.

Apple Watch Live Photo:

- Identify Live Photos by the icon in the bottom left corner.
- Touch and hold a Live Photo to experience its dynamic content.

Share your photo:

1. While viewing a photo, tap the Actions button.
2. Select a sharing option to seamlessly share your captured moments.

Create a watch face with a photo:

1. While viewing a photo, tap the Actions button.

2. Scroll down and tap Create Face.

3. Alternatively, you can use the Apple Watch app on your iPhone to create a Kaleidoscope watch face or add a new photo watch face.

4. For further customization, explore the options for Change the Apple Watch Face.

Pro Tip: *You can easily create a watch face on your iPhone with a few simple steps in the Photos app.*

Sleep: Master Sleep Tracking with Apple Watch

The Sleep app on Apple Watch lets you create an effective sleep schedule, monitor your sleep stages, and gain valuable insight into your sleep patterns.

Start sleep tracking:

1. Open the Sleep app on your Apple Watch.

2. Follow the on-screen instructions to set your sleep schedule.

3. For accurate sleep tracking, please wear the watch to bed.

4. After you wake up, open your sleep app and assess your sleep time and trends over the past 14 days.

Use Siri:

- Ask Siri questions like "How much sleep did you get last night?" on Apple Watch Series 9 (watchOS 10.2+) (availability varies by language and region).

Battery management:

- If your watch has less than 30% charge before bed, you will be prompted to charge it. In the morning, check the charging status based on the greeting.

Create multiple schedules:

- Create diverse schedules for weekdays and weekends.

- Set sleep goals, bedtimes, wake-up times, and alarm sounds for each schedule.

- Enable Sleep Focus to minimize distractions before bed and protect your sleep.

Note: For accurate data, please make sure you sleep at least 4 hours each night.

Sleep app navigation:

1. Press and hold the Digital Crown to access Control Center, then tap the

Sleep Focus button to turn off Sleep

Focus.

2. Set sleep mode on your Apple

Watch.

Alternatively, you can set it up using the

Health app on your iPhone. **Manage**

alarms and schedules:

1. Open the Sleep app.

2. Tap Alarm to adjust or turn

off the alarm.

3. Edit your schedule from Sleep

> Schedule in the Health app

on your iPhone.

Change sleep options:

1. Open the Settings app on your Apple Watch.

2. Tap Sleep.

3. Customize options such as "Turn on when relaxing", "Sleep screen", "Display time", "Sleep tracking", "Charging reminder", etc.

Check your sleep history:

2. Open the Sleep app on your Apple Watch to see your nightly sleep time, sleep stages, and average sleep time over 14 days.

3. Access your detailed sleep history in the Health app on iPhone under Browse > Sleep.

Respiration rate monitoring:

4. Track your breathing rate while you sleep to gain insight into your health. - Check the data in the iPhone Health app under Browse > Respiratory.

Disable respiration rate measurement:

1. Open the Settings app on your Apple Watch.

2. Go to Privacy & Security > Health.

3. Turn off breathing rate.

4. Alternatively, you can turn it off in the Apple Watch app on your iPhone under My Watch > Privacy.

Optimize your sleep habits and improve your overall health with sleep tracking on Apple Watch.

Stopwatch: Master the Stopwatch Feature

Easily track events and track lap and split times with your Apple Watch. Achieve precision and convenience with a stopwatch app that offers format flexibility and integration with specific watch faces.

Activate stopwatch:

1. Open the Stopwatch app on your Apple Watch or tap the stopwatch icon on the watch face (available on Chronograph or Chronograph Pro watches).

2. Use the Digital Crown to select analog, hybrid, or digital format.

Stopwatch function control:

5. Start: Tap the "Start" button.

6. Record a lap: Tap the lap button.

7. Recording end time: Tap the "Stop" button.

8. Reset the stopwatch: When the watch is stopped, tap the "Reset" button.

Note: *The timer will continue to work even if you return to the watch face or use another app.*

Select a display format:

9. Customize your stopwatch display by selecting analog, hybrid, or digital format with the Digital Crown.

Evaluation results:

10. Examine timing results in the display format of your choice.

11. Switch between displays to analyze your lap times, identify your fastest laps (green) and slowest laps (red), and gain insight into your performance.

Enhance your timekeeping experience on Apple Watch, leveraging the convenience of the Stopwatch app and seamless integration with specific watch faces for a customized and efficient tracking process.

Tips: Unlock Insights About Your Apple Watch

Explore a curated collection of insightful tips in the Tips app to unlock the full potential of your Apple Watch. Improve your watchOS experience, discover hidden features, and master customization with ease.

Access tips:

1. Go to the Tips app on your Apple Watch.
2. Explore different collections and discover the rich features that watchOS has to offer.

Browsing tips:

1. Tap on the tip collection and easily scroll down to absorb the valuable content of each tip.

2. Click the "Repeat" button to watch the animation again to get animation hints.

3. If a tip has a "Try" button, tap it to see the tip working on your Apple Watch.

4. Scroll down to move seamlessly to the next tip.

Tips: *Get instant access to the latest tips to stay informed. Integrate the Tips widget into your smart stack and add Tips complications to your watch face.*

Wallet: Explore Wallet on Apple Watch

Use the power of the Wallet app on Apple Watch to centralize and seamlessly access your cards and passes. Wallets efficiently manage many factors, including:

- Apple Pay cards such as Apple Card and Apple Cash

- Public transport map

- Digital key

- Driver's license or state ID card (US only)

- Student card

- Point cards, boarding passes, event tickets
- Vaccination records

Seamlessly manage your finances on Apple Watch (US only)

Easily send, receive, and send money using Apple Cash on your Apple Watch. This is only available in the US. Simplify your financial transactions with these simple steps.

Send payment:

1. Activate Siri and say something like, "Send Claire $25." If you have multiple Claires in your contacts,

select a specific Claire from among them.

2. Open the Messages app on your Apple Watch.

3. Tap the app button during a conversation and select the Apple Cash option.

4. Use the digital crown or button to select the whole dollar amount.

5. For amounts that are not whole dollar amounts (for example, $10.95), tap the amount, adjust the decimal point, and use the Digital Crown to set the value.

6. Double-click the side button to confirm and submit your payment.

Cancel payment:

Pending payments can be canceled unless the recipient approves.

- Go to the Wallet app on your Apple Watch, select your card, search for outstanding transactions, and cancel them.

Payment Request:

1. Use Siri to issue a command such as "I'd like Nisha to send me $30."
2. In the Messages app, tap Apple Cash, swipe left on Send, enter the amount, then tap Request.

Reply to payment request:

- In the message payment request, tap the "Send" button, adjust the amount if necessary, and double-click the side button to complete the payment.

Transaction details:

- Open the app on your Apple Watch to see transaction summaries in Messages.
- In the Wallet app, tap a card and scroll through the list to see specific card transactions.
- Access your iPhone's comprehensive history by opening the Apple Watch app, going to

Wallet and Apple Pay, and viewing your Apple Cash transactions. For detailed transaction history, request a PDF statement via email.

Weather: Get Weather Updates

The Weather app on Apple Watch makes it easy to track current and upcoming weather conditions. Whether you're interested in local weather or global weather forecasts, this app provides a comprehensive overview, including:

- Current temperature
- Sky conditions (sunny, cloudy, etc.)

- Daily minimum and maximum
  temperatures
- Rainfall details
- wind speed
- UV index
- visibility
- Humidity
- Air quality (availability may vary by
  location)

Easy weather check with Siri:

Quickly ask Siri about the weather by
saying commands like "What's the
weather?" "What's the weather forecast
for Honolulu tomorrow?"

Check your local weather:

Turn on Location Services to see local weather on your Apple Watch. Open the Settings app, go to Privacy & Security, and tap Location Services to turn it on. On your iPhone, go to Settings > Privacy & Security > Location Services > Weather and select an option.

Show weather forecast:

1. Open the Weather app on your Apple Watch.
2. Scroll down to see the 24-hour forecast with detailed conditions and temperatures.

3. For a detailed outlook, scroll down on another screen to access the 10-day forecast.

Detailed weather indicators:

Look at specific weather indicators like temperature, humidity, and air quality individually.

1. Tap the "Weather Conditions" button on the top right.

2. Select a metric.

3. Use the Digital Crown to view forecast details for that particular metric.

4. Tap the display to scroll through the available measurements.

Weather advice:

Notifications appear at the top of the Weather app to keep you up to date on important weather events. Tap Details to access more details. Please note that weather forecasts are not available in all locations.

Workout: Discover The Latest Workout Features

Explore watchOS 10's expanded workout features through the Workout app on Apple Watch. These updates include:

1. Cycling Improvements:

- Automatically connect to Bluetooth-enabled accessories and receive additional cadence and power data during your cycling training.

2. Training view on iPhone:

- Start a bike workout on your watch and it seamlessly appears as a live activity on your iPhone.
- Tap an activity on your iPhone to view it in full-screen mode, optimizing visibility of key metrics during your ride.

3. Performance Zone:

- Monitor your cycling intensity by connecting to a Bluetooth-enabled power meter and visualizing power zones on your Apple Watch.

4. Functional Threshold Performance:

- Access your Functional Threshold Power estimate of your best sustained strength over an hour directly from the Health app on your iPhone.

5. New training view:

- Enjoy different training experiences with updated training views.

- Rotate the Digital Crown to get a new perspective on metrics such as power zones, cadence, riding power and riding speed.

6. Golf Improvements (Apple Watch Series 8 and Series 9):

- During golf practice, the watch automatically detects when you are riding in a golf cart and provides more accurate calorie readings. Stay ahead of your fitness journey with these innovative workout features tailored to enhance your cycling and golf experiences on Apple Watch.

World Clock: Explore The World's Time Zones

The World Clock app on Apple Watch makes it easy to check the time in different cities around the world.

Siri:

Simplify the process by saying things like "What time is it in Oakland?"

Add and remove cities to world clock:

1. Open the World Clock app on your Apple Watch.
2. Tap the List button and select Add to add a new city.

3. Enter the city name by hand or dictation.

    - For Scribble, swipe up from the bottom of the screen and tap Scribble (may not be available in all languages).

4. Tap the city name to add it to your world clock.

5. Swipe left on the city name in the list and tap the X to remove it.

Tips: Cities you add to your iPhone also appear in the world clock on your Apple Watch.

Check time in another city:

1. Open the World Clock app on your Apple Watch.

2. Tap the List button and use the Digital Crown or swipe to move through the list.

3. To access a city's details, tap its name in the list.

4. Tap the back button or swipe right to return to the city list.

Tips: To quickly access the time in a specific city, consider adding a world clock complication to your watch face.

Change city abbreviation:

1. Open the Apple Watch app on your iPhone.

2. Go to My Watch and go to Watch > City Abbreviations.

3. Tap the city whose abbreviation you want to change.

APPLE WATCH ACCESSIBILITY

Improve Accessibility with Voice Over on Apple Watch

Voice Over is a powerful tool that enhances your Apple Watch experience with simple gestures and spoken navigation for navigation.

Enable or disable Voice Over:

1. Open the Settings app on your Apple Watch.

2. Go to Accessibility > Voice Over and turn on Voice Over.

3. Double-tap the Voice Over button to turn it off.

Siri: "Turn on Voice Over" or "Turn off Voice Over."

Alternatively, you can manage his Voice Over settings on your iPhone by going to the Apple Watch app, tapping My Watch, selecting Accessibility, and selecting the Voice Over option. You can also use accessibility shortcuts.

Use Voice Over during setup:

- Triple-click the Digital Crown during Apple Watch setup to enable Voice Over.

Explore Voice Over gestures:

Navigate:

- Move your finger across the display to hear the item's name read out loud. Tap once to select, swipe left or right to see adjacent items, or use two fingers to browse other pages.

Back:

- Perform a two-finger scrubbing motion (tracing a "Z" shape) to undo the step.

Actions on items:

- Double tap to open an app or perform an action. For example, double tap to turn off his Voice Over.

Additional actions:

- Swipe up or down to select one of the available actions and double tap to perform it.

Pause reading:

- Tap the screen with two fingers to pause Voice Over, then repeat to continue.

Adjust volume:

- Double tap and hold with two fingers, then swipe up or down. Alternatively, you can adjust it in the Apple Watch app under Accessibility > Voice Over.

Voice Over hand gestures:

- Turn on hand gestures in the Apple Watch app to replace taps with hand gestures. Control Voice Over by pinching, double-tap, tap, and double-tap.

Note: The universal double-tap gesture on Apple Watch Series 9 is not available with Voice Over hand gestures.

Use the Voice Over rotor to navigate:

- Use the rotor to change settings and toggle items. Rotate two fingers on the screen to select words, characters, actions, headings, volume, and speaking speed.

Adjust Voice Over settings:

Access his Voice Over settings on your Apple Watch.

1. Open the Settings app.
2. Go to Accessibility > Voice Over.

Options include:

- Turn off Voice Over.
- Adjust speaking speed.
- Set audio options for voice, pitch and rotor language.
- Set audio options for volume, audio ducking, sound, adjust audio volume and haptics.

- Configure output, input, line
  wrapping, alarm display duration
  and table braille options.

- Manage keyboard options for paired
  Bluetooth keyboards, including
  voice feedback, typing feedback,
  modifier keys, keyboard interaction
  time, and devices.

- Disable Voice Over hints.

- Navigate using the Digital Crown.

- Raise your wrist to hear the name of
  the highlighted item.

- Enable screen curtain for increased
  privacy.

- Enable countdown.

- Set hand gestures.

Improved interaction with Assistive Touch on Apple Watch

Assistive Touch enables a more accessible and user-friendly experience on Apple Watch. This feature supports users who have difficulty using touch or buttons, and allows control using hand gestures.

Enable Assistive Touch:

1. Open the Settings app on your Apple Watch.

2. Go to Accessibility > Assistive Touch and turn on Assistive Touch.

3. Enable hand gestures for better control.

Siri: "Please turn on Assistive Touch."

Alternatively, you can manage Assistive Touch settings on your iPhone through the Apple Watch app by tapping My Watch, going to Accessibility > Assistive Touch, and turning on Assistive Touch.

Perform actions with hand gestures:

Use gestures to perform various actions on your Apple Watch, including: Typing, swiping, etc. Actions include tapping the display, pressing and rotating the Digital Crown, swiping between screens, accessing Notification Center, using Apple Pay, and more.

Note: The universal double-tap gesture on Apple Watch Series 9 is not available with Assistive Touch.

Set up Assistive Touch:

1. Open the Settings app on your Apple Watch.
2. Go to Accessibility > Assistive Touch and enable Assistive Touch.
3. Tap Hand Gestures to enable hand gestures.

Tip: Tap More below the hand gestures switch to learn hand gestures.

Use Assistive Touch with standard gestures:

When you enable Assistive Touch and hand gestures, you can use standard gestures to interact with your Apple Watch.

- Pinch: forward
- Double pinch: back
- Refine: Tap
- Double squeeze: Display action menu

Example: Use Assistive Touch to interact with the Activity app.

1. Squeeze to activate Assistive Touch.

2. Pinch three times to go to Add Activities, then pinch and tap.

3. Squeeze the air twice and an action menu will appear.

4. Use pinch and press to navigate the action.

Discover motion pointers:

In addition to pinching and pressing, Motion Pointer lets you control your Apple Watch by tilting it up, down, left, or right. Interact with the app, scroll, and interact with the motion pointer.

Quick actions for notifications:

Quick actions allow you to respond quickly to alerts. For example, press twice to answer an incoming call. Customize quick actions in the Settings app under Accessibility > Quick Actions.

Adjust Assistive Touch settings:

1. Open the Settings app on your Apple Watch.

2. Go to Accessibility > Assistive Touch.

Customization options:

- Tap "Hand Gestures" to customize your gestures.

- Adjust settings such as motion pointer sensitivity.

- Choose between automatic and manual scanning styles.

- Improve visibility with high contrast or different highlight colors.

- Personalize your menu with your favorite actions, position, size adjustment, and automatic scroll speed.

- Confirm your payment with Assistive Touch.

Tips: *Explore these settings to adjust your Assistive Touch to suit your preferences and needs for a seamless Apple Watch experience.*

Improved Visual Settings for Better Accessibility on Apple Watch

Customize the visual settings of your Apple Watch to your liking and improve your interactions with on-screen elements. Adjust text size and various display options for a personalized and user-friendly experience.

Adjust text size:

1. Press the side button to open Control Center.

2. Tap the "Adjust font size" button.

3. Rotate the Digital Crown to adjust the font size to your liking.

Change text and appearance:

Customize how text and other elements appear on your screen by adjusting the following settings in the Settings app:

On/Off Labels:

- Enable button labels to clearly identify enabled options.

Reduce transparency:

- Improve readability by reducing the transparency, especially of certain backgrounds.

Improved contrast:

- Improve the contrast between the app's foreground and background colors.

Color Filters:

- Use customizable color filters to support people who are colorblind or have trouble reading text.

Text Size:

- Adjust the overall size of the text for easier reading.

Bold Text:

- Enable bold text for extra emphasis.

Note: *Bold and grayscale changes require a restart to fully implement. To adjust these settings, use the Apple Watch app on your iPhone.*

Animation limitations:

Minimize motion effects on the home screen and when opening and closing apps to reduce visual irritation.

1. Open the Settings app on your Apple Watch.
2. Go to Accessibility > Reduce movement.
3. Check "Reduce Motion" to limit the animation effect.

Tip: *To maintain consistent app icon sizes on your home screen, combine Reduce Motion with grid view.*

Use Siri for Accessibility Features on Apple Watch

Use Siri to seamlessly integrate accessibility features into your Apple Watch experience. Siri makes it easy to open apps, toggle different settings, and use intelligent features as your virtual assistant.

Siri command:

Start accessibility features with Siri using a command like the following:

- "Please turn on Voice Over."

- "Please turn off Voice Over."

Siri is set to Voice Over status and often provides more information verbally than what is displayed on screen. Additionally, you can use Voice Over to interpret Siri's responses audibly.

Adjust Siri response time:

1. Open the Settings app on your Apple Watch.

2. Go to Accessibility > Siri.

3. Scroll down and select Standard, Long, or Longest for Siri Pause Time.

Type instead of speak:

To decide whether to type Siri requests instead of speaking them, follow these steps:

1. Open the Settings app on your Apple Watch.
2. Go to Accessibility > Siri.
3. Enable input to Siri.

Tips: Improve your accessibility experience on Apple Watch by seamlessly integrating the voice and input capabilities of Siri to meet your unique needs.

Apple Watch Accessibility Shortcut Settings

Digital Crown makes it easy to turn key accessibility features on or off with just a triple-click. Enhance your Apple Watch experience by enabling or disabling features like Assistive Touch, Nearby Device Control, Lateral Balance, Motion Reduction, Transparency Reduction, Touch Accommodations, Voice Over, and Zoom.

Set up accessibility shortcuts:

1. Open the Settings app on your Apple Watch.

2. Go to Accessibility > Accessibility Shortcuts.

3. Tap to highlight the feature you want to include in your shortcut.

Alternatively, in the Apple Watch app on your iPhone, go to My Watch > Accessibility > Accessibility Shortcuts and make your selection.

Please use shortcut:

Click the Digital Crown three times quickly to start the shortcut.

If multiple functions are linked,

1. Select a specific feature.

2. Tap Done.

Tips: *Triple-clicking the Digital Crown again will seamlessly disable the selected accessibility features. Streamline your interactions with Apple Watch with these quick and customizable accessibility shortcuts.*

RESTART, RESTORE AND MORE...

Restart your Apple Watch:

If you're having trouble with your Apple Watch, consider restarting both your Apple Watch and your paired iPhone. Perform the following steps:

1. Turn off your Apple Watch: Press and hold the side button until the slider appears. Tap the power button and drag the power off slider to the right.

2. Turn on your Apple Watch: Press and hold the side button until you see the Apple logo.

Note: *You cannot restart your Apple Watch while it is charging.*

Restart your paired iPhone:

To perform a complete restart, turn off your paired iPhone and then turn it back on.

1. Turn off your iPhone.

- For Face ID models, press and hold the side button and volume button. Drag the slider to the right.

- For models without Face ID, press and hold the side or top button until the slider appears. Drag the slider to the right.

- Alternatively, go to Settings > General > Shutdown.

2. Turn on your iPhone. Press and hold the Side or Top button until you see the Apple logo.

Force restart your Apple Watch:

If you can't turn off your Apple Watch or the issue persists, try a force restart.

- Press and hold the side button and digital crown at the same time for at least 10 seconds. Let go when you see the Apple logo.

Unpair And Remove Your Apple Watch

If you want to remove content and settings from your Apple Watch, you have two options:

1. Unpair your Apple Watch:

Unpairing your Apple Watch and iPhone is useful if you want to delete content and remove activation locks so you can sell or give it away.

- Open the Apple Watch app on your iPhone.
- Tap "My Watches" and select "All Watches".

- Tap the Info button next to your watch and choose Unpair Apple Watch.

After you complete these steps, your Apple Watch will be erased and removed from your iCloud account, Activation Lock will be disabled, and it will be ready for a new setup.

2. Clear your Apple Watch and settings:

If you need to hold your Apple Watch and reset it, follow these steps.

- Open the Settings app on your Apple Watch.

- Go to General > Reset, tap Erase all content and settings, and enter your passcode.

- For cellular-enabled watches, decide whether to keep or remove your cellular plan.

After this process, set up your Apple Watch again. When prompted, choose to restore from backup.

Note: If you forget your passcode and can't access the Settings app, you'll need to reset it.

Delete cell phone plan:

If your Apple Watch has cellular capabilities, you can remove your cellular plan at any time.

- Open the Apple Watch app on your iPhone.

- Tap My Watch, go to Cellular, and select the About button next to your cellular plan.

- Select "Delete [provider name] plan" and confirm your decision.

Note: *You may need to contact your mobile phone provider to complete the deletion.*

Reset Your Apple Watch Passcode

If you forget your Apple Watch passcode, or if it's deactivated after multiple failed attempts, you can reset your Apple Watch or your paired iPhone to set it up again.

Important: If you enable wipe data, your data will be deleted after 10 failed passcode attempts.

Reset from Apple Watch:

1. Place your Apple Watch on the charger and press and hold the side button until the slider appears.

2. Press and hold the Digital Crown until the Erase All Content and Settings screen appears.

3. Tap Reset, then tap Reset again to confirm.

4. Once completed, continue with setup. Restore from your backup when prompted.

Reset on paired iPhone:

1. Open the Apple Watch app on your iPhone and go to My Watch.

2. Tap General, scroll down and select Reset.

3. Select Erase Apple Watch Content and Settings, then tap Erase All Content and Settings to confirm.

4. For cell phone-enabled watches, decide whether to keep or remove your cell phone plan.

   - If you want to pair your Apple Watch and iPhone again, keep your plans.

   - Delete your plan if you want to pair it with another iPhone or cancel your cell phone contract.

5. Once the process is complete, set up your watch again and restore from your backup when prompted.

Note: *This method enables Activation Lock. You need an Apple ID and password to unpair, pair with a new iPhone, turn off Find My on your device, and more.*

Apple Watch Recovery Instructions

If your Apple Watch displays an animation depicting the watch and a nearby iPhone, follow these recovery steps.

1. Place your iPhone near your Apple Watch.

2. Make sure your iPhone is running iOS 15.4 or later, Bluetooth enabled, connected to Wi-Fi, and currently unlocked.

3. Place your Apple Watch on the charging dock.

4. Double-click the side button on your Apple Watch and follow the instructions on your iPhone.

Restore Your Apple Watch Using Your Backup

Your Apple Watch automatically backs up to your paired iPhone, allowing for a seamless restore process. Backups are built into your iPhone's entire backup system, whether they're stored in iCloud or on your Mac/PC. Note that backups stored in iCloud cannot be viewed directly.

Apple Watch backup and restore:

1. **Back up your Apple Watch:** It's easy to continuously back up your Apple Watch content to your paired iPhone. Once you unpair your device, the backup will start automatically.

2. **Restore from Backup:** If you want to re-pair your Apple Watch with the same iPhone or buy a new

Apple Watch, select Restore from
Backup to restore the backup stored
on your iPhone. You can choose
from.

For family-managed Apple Watches:

To prevent iCloud backups on your
managed watch, go to the Settings app on
your managed Apple Watch, go to
[account name] > iCloud > iCloud
Backup, and turn off iCloud backup.

Update Your Apple Watch Software

Follow these steps in the Apple Watch
app on your iPhone to make sure your

Apple Watch is running the latest

software version.

Check for and install software

updates:

1. Open the Apple Watch app on your

   iPhone.

2. Go to My Watch and select General.

3. Tap "Software Update". If an update

   is available, select Download and

   Install.

Alternative method:

1. Open the Settings app on your

   Apple Watch.

2. Go to General and select Software Update.

Tips: *Keeping your Apple Watch software up to date helps you stay up to date with the latest features and improvements.*

TIPS AND STRATEGIES

Secure A Misplaced Apple Watch

If your Apple Watch is misplaced, you can activate Lost Mode.

Locate Your Apple Watch:

1. Launch the Apple Watch app on your iPhone.

2. Navigate to "My Watch" and select "All Watches."

3. Tap the Info button next to your watch and choose "Find My Apple Watch."

4. In the Find My app on your iPhone, locate your watch on the map.

5. If it's in your vicinity, select "Play Sound" for an audible alert.

Mark Apple Watch as Lost:

When marked as lost, your watch is secured with a passcode, protecting personal data and suspending Apple Pay.

1. Open the Apple Watch app on your iPhone.

2. Tap "My Watch" and select "All Watches."

3. Tap the Info button next to your watch and choose "Find My Apple Watch."

4. In the Find My app on your iPhone, tap "Activate" under "Mark As Lost" and continue.

5. Enter a contact phone number for the finder.

6. Next, input a message to display on your Apple Watch.

7. Tap "Activate" to mark the watch as lost.

Erase a Misplaced Apple Watch:

Before erasing, attempt to locate or activate a sound. Once erased, locating or sounding alerts is not possible.

1. Open the Apple Watch app on your iPhone.

2. Tap "My Watch" and select "All Watches."

3. Tap the Info button next to your watch and choose "Find My Apple Watch."

4. In the Find My app on your iPhone, tap your watch and then tap "Erase This Device."

Remove Payment Cards Remotely:

In case of loss or theft, sign in to appleid.apple.com to remove cards.

1. Access appleid.apple.com using your Apple ID.

2. In the Devices section, select your Apple Watch.

3. Click "Remove Items" under Wallet & Apple Pay, then confirm.

Alternatively, contact your card issuers.

Note: *If your Apple Watch and iPhone are disconnected or malfunctioning, erase the watch's content first and then unpair it using the Apple Watch app on your iPhone (if possible).*

Unlock Your iPhone With Apple Watch

Activate your Apple Watch to unlock your girlfriend's iPhone for Siri commands or if you have trouble recognizing her face with Face ID. Perform the following steps:

1. On your iPhone, go to Settings > Face ID & Passcode and enter your passcode.

2. Scroll down to Unlock with Apple Watch and enable settings for your specific watch.

3. If you have multiple watches, enable the settings for each one.

Apple Watch lets you know your iPhone has been successfully unlocked with a quick tap on your wrist.

Note: *To unlock your iPhone, your Apple Watch must have a valid passcode, be* *unlocked, on your wrist, and near your iPhone.*

Unlock Your Mac with Apple Watch

If you have a mid-2013 or newer Mac running macOS 10.13 or later, you can enable Seamless Unlock on your Apple Watch when your Mac exits sleep mode. The prerequisite is that both your Mac and Apple Watch are signed into iCloud with the same Apple ID.

Pro Tip: *To find the model year of your Mac, click the Apple menu in the top-left corner of your screen, choose About This*

Mac, and find the year next to the model

description (e.g.: "MacBook Pro (15-inch,

2018)").

Enable auto-unlock:

Make sure the following configurations
are set:

1. Wi-Fi and Bluetooth are enabled on
   your Mac.
2. Both your Mac and Apple Watch
   sign in to iCloud with the same
   Apple ID and use two-factor
   authentication.
3. Apple Watch is passcode protected.

Then, follow these steps:

- For macOS 13 or later, go to Apple
  Menu > System Preferences and
  click Sign-in Password.
- For macOS 12 or earlier, go to Apple
  Menu > System Preferences, select
  Security & Privacy, then click
  General.

Check the "Use Apple Watch to unlock
apps and Mac" box.

- If you have multiple Apple Watches,
  choose the specific Apple Watch you
  want to use to unlock your Mac and
  apps.
- If two-factor authentication isn't
  enabled for your Apple ID, follow

the onscreen instructions and try

checking the box again.

Unlock your Mac:

Once your Apple Watch is on your wrist

and unlocked, you can easily start your

Mac without entering a password. Make

sure your Apple Watch is close to your

Mac.

SAFETY GUIDELINES FOR USING APPLE WATCH

Warning: Failure to follow these safety precautions may result in fire, electric shock, personal injury, or damage to your Apple Watch or other property. Read and understand all safety information before using Apple Watch.

Handling

Handle your Apple Watch with care, considering the different materials used in the case.

- Apple Watch aluminum case: 7000 series aluminum, Ion-X glass, composite (plastic) back

- Stainless Steel Apple Watch Case: Stainless steel, sapphire crystal, ceramic back

- Apple Watch Titanium Case: Titanium, sapphire crystal, ceramic back

- Ceramic Apple Watch Case: Ceramic, Sapphire Crystal, Ceramic Back

Apple Watch contains sensitive electronic components that can be damaged by drops, burns, punctures, or crushes. Ceramic cases can chip or crack if subjected to strong influences. Do not use a damaged Apple Watch as it may cause injury. Do not expose to dust or sand for a long time.

Repair

Don't try to open or repair Apple Watch yourself. Doing so may cause damage, loss of water resistance, and injury. If your device is damaged or malfunctioning, contact Apple or your authorized service provider.

Battery

Avoid replacing your Apple Watch battery yourself. Improper handling may cause overheating and injury. Battery maintenance must be performed only by Apple or an authorized service provider. Batteries must be recycled separately from household waste.

Distraction

Using Apple Watch in certain situations can be distracting and potentially dangerous. Follow rules that limit the use of mobile devices, especially during activities that require your full attention.

Navigation

Maps and location-based apps rely on data services. Please note that the Service may be unavailable, inaccurate or incomplete. Compare information on your Apple Watch to information around you, pay attention to traffic signs, and avoid using your Apple Watch during activities that require your full attention.

Charging

Apple Watch charges using a power adapter that is compatible with Apple's magnetic charging accessories. Third-party adapters must meet safety standards. Using a damaged cable or charger or charging when wet can be dangerous. Ensure adequate ventilation during use or charging. ***Prolonged exposure to heat***

Although Apple Watch respects temperature limits, prolonged contact with warm surfaces can cause discomfort or injury. Please be careful when using or charging and avoid prolonged skin contact.

Hearing loss

Loud volumes can damage your hearing. Prioritize safe audio levels and check the volume before using a Bluetooth-connected headset.

Warning: Avoid prolonged exposure to high volume levels.

Radio Frequency Exposure

Apple Watch uses radio signals for wireless connectivity. See the Apple Watch app for information on how to minimize your exposure to radio frequencies.

Radio Frequency Interference

Be aware of signs prohibiting the use of electronic devices, as emissions from Apple Watch and charging accessories can affect other devices. Use airplane mode in restricted areas.

Medical device interference

Apple Watch contains magnets and emits electromagnetic fields. Consult your physician and medical device manufacturer regarding possible interference. Keep a safe distance from medical equipment.

Not a medical device

Apple Watch is not a medical device and should not replace professional medical judgment. Consult your health care provider before making any health-related decisions.

Disease

Consult your doctor before starting or changing an exercise program using Apple Watch. Be careful while exercising, stop if you experience discomfort, and assume your risk.

Explosive and atmospheric conditions

Do not charge or use Apple Watch in a potentially explosive atmosphere. Exposure to high concentrations of chemicals can impair functionality. Please follow all signs and instructions.

Activities with significant impact

Apple Watch is not suitable for activities where device failure could have serious consequences.

Suffocation Hazard

Certain Apple Watch bands can pose a choking hazard for young children. Please stay away from them.

Skin sensitivity

Use caution if you experience skin intolerance. Keep it clean and dry to reduce the risk of irritation. If irritation persists, consult your doctor. **Nickel exposure**

Some materials in Apple Watch contain trace amounts of nickel. People with nickel allergies should be careful.

Acrylates and methacrylates

Apple Watch and bracelets contain trace amounts of acrylates and methacrylates and meet safety standards. People who are sensitive to these substances should use caution.

Conclusion

Prioritize your security and follow these guidelines to use your Apple Watch safely.

Have fun using your smart watch.

www.ingramcontent.com/pod-product-compliance
Lightning Source LLC
LaVergne TN
LVHW051429050326
832903LV00030BD/2982